A History Of
POSTCARDS

Previous page: Art Deco glamour by Chilton Longley. The best postcards falling within the Art Deco classification, which reached its peak in the mid-1920s, are now highly prized by collectors in both America and Continental Europe.

A History Of POSTCARDS

A pictorial record
from the turn of the century to the present day

Martin Willoughby

Formerly of the Collector's Department, Phillips of London

STUDIO EDITIONS
LONDON

A History of Postcards

First published 1992 by Studio Editions Ltd.
Princess House, 50 Eastcastle Street
London W1N 7AP, England.

Copyright this edition © Studio Editions Ltd., 1992

ISBN 1-85170-422-1

Printed and bound in **Singapore**

CONTENTS

INTRODUCTION

The trouble with history is that, since it is an ongoing process, it cannot conveniently be divided up into sections. However, any book with those rather grand words 'The History of . . .' in its title is going to have to divide itself somehow into chronological 'chunks'. In the case of picture postcards, which have only been around for a little over a century, a great deal of activity has been squeezed into a fairly short space of time, but with much more happening during some periods than in others. Consequently, the 'chunks' tend to be of unequal length, some covering just a few years, others encompassing several decades.

For most people the summer vacation is a time of the year when a particular ritual has to be carried out, a ritual they will not have performed since the last holiday and will not do so again until the next: the sending of picture postcards to friends and relatives. It is a strange ritual, perhaps, just a few lines jotted down on the back of a colour photograph, to show the recipient that they have not been forgotten and to prove that the sender has actually gone somewhere exciting. However, this ritual has its origins in another age—historically not so long ago, but a time when sending postcards was so popular, indeed on the verge of an international addiction, that the seaside-holiday variety was just the tip of the iceberg.

For those who send, at most, maybe half a dozen postcards per year, it is difficult to imagine the enormous quantities of these little rectangular pieces of card that were winging their way in all directions through the world's postal systems at the height of their popularity. The postal authorities who produced the first rather drab, plain 'postal' or 'correspondence-cards' doubtless could not have foreseen the extent to which their basic ideas would be grasped and developed – evolving, within a couple of decades, into items that would be recognized and used by everyone the world over.

The postcard is a relatively recent phenomenon. Although a line of descent can be traced back through early pictorial

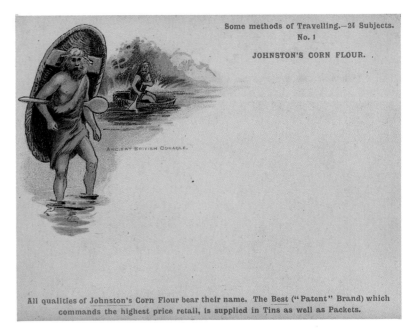

Left: A fine example of a postcard printed by chromolithography, depicting a tourist of the 1890s. Foreign travel no longer being a pastime exclusive to the very wealthy, tourists accounted for a high proportion of card sales in the late nineteenth century.

Above: A 'court' size card of 1897, No. 1 in a series of 24, depicting ancient and modern methods of travelling.

An official postcard issued by the government of Victoria, Australia, used in 1898. Note it was originally intended only for use 'For the United Kingdom, By the long sea route'!

A souvenir of the Paris Exposition of 1900, probably the most thoroughly covered event to be shown on picture postcards of its time.

Edward VII, 1902, the last card in the superb 'King & Queens of England' series published by Raphael Tuck & Sons Ltd. Thirty-seven were issued in all, comprising three sets of twelve (series numbers 614–616) and a final card for the new king, shown here.

Some of the most beautiful postcards ever published fall into the Art Nouveau category. This example is of c.1902. The flowing, graceful elegance of the images puts such examples into the realms of fine art, with, in most cases, correspondingly higher than average prices asked for them.

'London Life – The Bus Driver', used as a self-promotional card by Raphael Tuck & Sons Ltd. The reverse states that 'Tucks postcards are now a household word, and are welcomed and appreciated everywhere. No expense is spared in securing original design, the finest views, the most finished paintings, and their reproduction by the very best methods'.

trade cards, decorative hand-drawn and -printed envelopes, visiting cards and carte-de-visite photographs, it was not until the late 1860s that the first officially produced postcard went on sale. Although initially the card was not welcomed by everyone, its advantages (being cheaper to send than a letter, and saving the need to buy writing paper and envelopes) ensured that the idea was popular enough to catch on. Also, businessmen realized the potential of such cards to advertise their products, and privately printed publicity cards were among the first to bear pictorial vignettes.

Through various changes in postal regulations, and the development of improved, cost-effective colour-printing techniques, it only took a few years' work to transform the postcard into a mass-produced, readily available, full-colour souvenir of almost universal acceptance. The 1890s saw the blossoming of the *Gruss aus . . .* or 'Greetings from . . .' cards, depicting two or three small colour views of a particular town, with room for a few words of greeting.

Postcards were not just sent as holiday souvenirs. By the turn of the century, the 'golden age' of the postcard had truly

begun and the holiday-view card became only one of the hundreds of different types available, with hundreds of different reasons for sending them. Postcards depicting birthday and Christmas greetings, actresses, ships, railway engines, animals, military leaders, royalty, comical scenes, and the works of leading artists started to appear in the shops, and the more widespread and interesting the subject matter, the more people took an interest in them. Soon a person did not need a particular reason to send a postcard to a friend—the picture was reason enough and if you were lucky, the recipient might send one in return.

The next instalment in the postcard story is obvious: they began to be collected. Being bright, decorative objects that could be gathered together in one place and easily stored, postcards became an ideal collectible. It would seem that no sooner had the first picture postcard dropped through its first letterbox onto its first doormat, than the first postcard album was produced to put it in. The previous generation had had albums in which to keep their family portrait photographs, so the postcard album was a natural successor. From the richest house-

holds to the poorest, postcard albums were eagerly filled the world over. Even Queen Victoria decided that it was time to start a royal collection.

However, it is difficult to discern whether postcard collecting was a result of the increase in the use of postcards or whether the increase in their use came about because people started collecting them. The extremely large quantities in use were proof of how popular they had become, but there were several practical reasons, as well as the purely pleasurable ones, for this usage. For the general public, the postcard was initially a cost-cutting device. Most postcards were cheap to purchase, certainly cheaper than buying envelopes and sheets of writing paper, so therein was the first saving. Secondly, in the majority of countries a card cost approximately half as much to send as a standard letter (the large increase in mail made this viable from the Post Office's point of view). Initially, the savings had been even greater, for .the first official postal stationery cards had stamps pre-printed on them and included in the cost. For example, in Great Britain a card could be bought and sent for the all-inclusive price of half a penny, and in the United

Edwardian beauties, a popular subject with collectors, 1905.

Right: The gradual replacement of horse-drawn transport in favour of the motorized kind took place during the heyday of the postcard.

Below, left to right: Art Nouveau elegance by A. K. Macdonald, now very sought-after and consequently expensive.

States for one cent. But perhaps the greatest benefit of the new postcards was the saving in time they allowed. There always had been, and always would be, certain types of messages not suitable for writing on postcards, for instance personal and business letters, but there were many instances when a short note with very ordinary contents was all that was required. 'See you tomorrow at 4 p.m.', 'Caught last train, arrived home safely', birthday and Christmas greetings, business accounts and receipts were the types of correspondence for which the postcard was intended, and such messages could be written quickly and easily on the back of one of these small pieces of card and just dropped in a postbox.

There was also one other factor, taken for granted today, which might have stifled the development of the postcard had it been commonplace at the turn of the century: the telephone. These days it is the quickest, most readily available means of communication, of conveying a quick message. In 1900 it was not established in the households of the world, and therefore the postcard was, for most people, the quickest means of making contact with a friend, relative, or tradesman. The Post Office itself, of course, played its part in this. Collections were more frequent and sorting often continued during public holidays. Deliveries, too, were rapid and sometimes could occur within two or three hours of posting for mail sent between neighbouring towns and villages.

All these factors played a part in the extreme popularity of the picture postcard, a phenomenon whose golden age was to last for almost two decades. It was a time that saw much in the way of social change, and of technological and other advances, such as the development of the motor car and the aeroplane. Practically every aspect of Edwardian life was mirrored on postcards. The popularity of many actors and actresses of the day was almost directly due to the large numbers of cards depicting their portraits for sale in the shops. Politicians, military leaders, and sports figures all became more familiar to the public through the postcard, and the work of contemporary artists became known due to its appearance in postcard form.

The wide variety of subject matter on postcards included country views, comic scenes, pretty girls, children, animals, transportation, and military uniforms. For a short while the postcard had its heyday, being used by everyone and

Below: Covent Garden Flower Market, 1906; artist unknown.

Faint Heart.

Left: 'Faint Heart' by Ethel Parkinson, who painted many fine children's cards. This chromolithographic example was published, like the majority of her work, by C. W. Faulkner. Children have always been a popular subject with postcard publishers, hence the large numbers of cards depicting them still to be found, but the better artist-drawn examples are nevertheless eagerly collected.

Below: 'The Postman'. The message on the reverse simply says 'Now you have got a new album I thought you would like this card'. Postcard collecting was in full swing by 1906, the year this example was used.

The Postman

Above: A wonderful poster-type advertising card by Louis Wain, who was the undisputed master of painting cats in human situations.

Above right: 'One For The Governor', a cheeky Edwardian comic card.

Right: A fine series of these embossed cards, each depicting the postage stamps of a particular country, were published by Ottmar Zieher of Munich.

Left: 'The Devil Take These Postcards'; sentiments expressed by the few who were not enamoured of the latest craze. This initially included postmen, some of whom are believed to have expressed concern at the sudden increase in the amount of mail they had to deliver as a result of the popularity of the postcard.

Below left: No. 64 in the long series, 'The American Girl', painted by Alice Lueller Fidler.

welcomed in every household. Even during the First World War the flow of cards continued, although some of the more frivolous ones disappeared and patriotic types were the order of the day. It was not really until the end of World War I that the postcard boom ceased. There was a new mood of seriousness the world over, a mood into which the charms of the picture postcard did not fit. With the restructuring of postal systems, postage rates increased and the torrential flow of postcard mail was reduced to a trickle. But of course their history did not end at this point.

The 1920s brought new fashions, a novel approach to art (most notably the Art Deco style), and the blossoming of the motion-picture industry, whose stars replaced the earlier theatrical performers as best-sellers with the postcard-buying public. After the 1930s, however, production went into the doldrums again, with very little of notable interest to inspire a return to card mania.

It was not until the late 1960s that collecting started to pick up, but this time cards were sought out as historical artefacts, rather than as contemporary items. People started to realize that a whole past way of life was stored on the pages of old postcard albums, which could not be bettered as a chronicle of past times. The 1970s and 1980s witnessed the resurgence of postcard publishing as an art form in its own right, and currently there are many publishers in countries all over the globe that are producing fine designs reflecting the times we live in. The availability of such cards is becoming more widespread as their popularity increases, with many museums, art galleries, souvenir shops, bookshops, and stationers offering good selections. However, it is fairly certain we will never again reach the stage where, as in those few years either side of 1900, the craze for sending postcards took over the world.

Unusual novelty postcard c. 1907, employing a double-sided flap. With the flap up (above) the lady seems to be taking a bath—but when the flap is lowered (below) one sees that she is in fact being carried by two men and her knees are revealed as their bald heads! Publishers were always trying to come up with something different to stay ahead of the competition.

Some beautiful Art Deco designs were published during the 1920s. These examples, like so many, are of Italian origin. The work of a number of artists specializing in this style is now highly prized, but many fine unsigned, anonymous illustrations can still be found at a far more reasonable cost. Afghans and greyhounds often feature, the outline of their bodies suiting the style so well.

Left: The latest fashion: an Edwardian novelty comic card. The hat is made of real felt.

ONE OF THE H'ATTRACTIONS

Below: Embossed and gilded New Year greetings, 1906.

Below: Stylish Italian glamour by Tito Corbella.

A selection of collectable artist drawn cards. Clockwise from top left: Chromolithographic advertising vignette from just before the turn of the century; Greetings from the German mudbaths c.1902; Hold-to-Light greetings postcard—the words 'A Merry Christmas' appear to be illuminated when a strong light is placed behind the card; embossed American valentine c.1905; Chromolithographic dog, with the artist identified; a Write-Away; the beginning of a message was printed on such cards for completion by the sender, together with an appropriate illustration.

POSTAL REFORM: THE POSTCARD IS BORN

The development of pictorial printing, coupled with postal reform, created an environment during the second half of the nineteenth century in which the postcard was able to thrive. Indeed, if certain men had not explored the possibilities of establishing a cheaper rate of postage within a simpler postal system, and if their ideas had not been accepted, the postcard could never have evolved.

The initial breakthrough was in Great Britain in 1840 with the establishment of a uniform penny postage, prepaid by means of attaching a stamp to the outside of a folded letter or envelope. Before this date the postal system had been inefficient and expensive to run, and was the subject of much criticism as well. Rates for single letters were higher and were charged on the distance they had to be carried. These charges were usually collected from the recipient by the postman rather than paid in advance, and there was no guarantee that the addressee would agree to pay the required amount and accept the letter; indeed, in many cases they could not afford to. In addition, there was much free mail being carried, as certain groups of people such as Members of Parliament were allowed to send letters without charge (newspapers were similarly transported at no cost to the sender). The proportion of this unpaid mail within the postal system was fairly high, and the costs were borne by imposing higher-than-necessary rates on the general public's letters. The results were twofold: first, letter-writing never really took off, which tended to discourage the need for literacy among the poor and ill-educated, and second, trade was stifled, since the cost of sending business correspondence was prohibitive.

The solution was proposed in 1837 by a gentleman named Rowland Hill (1795-1879), who had previously been involved in educational reform and who for some years had been turning his attention to the problems of the postal

Above: Sir Henry Cole (1808–82), who assisted in the production of the Mulready postal stationery, and was responsible for the world's first Christmas card.

system. His ideas were based on simplifying the system and therefore bringing down the costs. He suggested that letters be charged not by distance carried, but by weight, and that a simple letter of less than half an ounce (14 grams) should be transported anywhere in the country for a standard charge, namely one penny. Hill also suggested that these charges be paid for in advance, either by buying official prepaid stationery or by sticking an adhesive label to the envelope (hence the postage stamp was first suggested). Rowland Hill's suggestions were published in a booklet entitled *Post Office Reform; Its Importance and Practicability,* privately printed by W. Clowes & Sons of Stamford Street, London, in 1837.

As he remarked, 'I early saw the terrible inconvenience of being poor . . . my mother was afraid the postman might bring a letter while she had no money to pay the postage'.

It took three years for various committees to analyze, accept, and finally implement Hill's ideas, but on 10 January 1840 the Uniform Penny Postage was finally introduced, thus paving the way for later developments such as the postcard. However, the relevance of the events of 1840 to the postcard do not end there. On 1 May of that year the first prepaid official Post Office envelopes were placed on sale, their purchase cost including the cost of postage and also the first postage, stamps ('Stamps

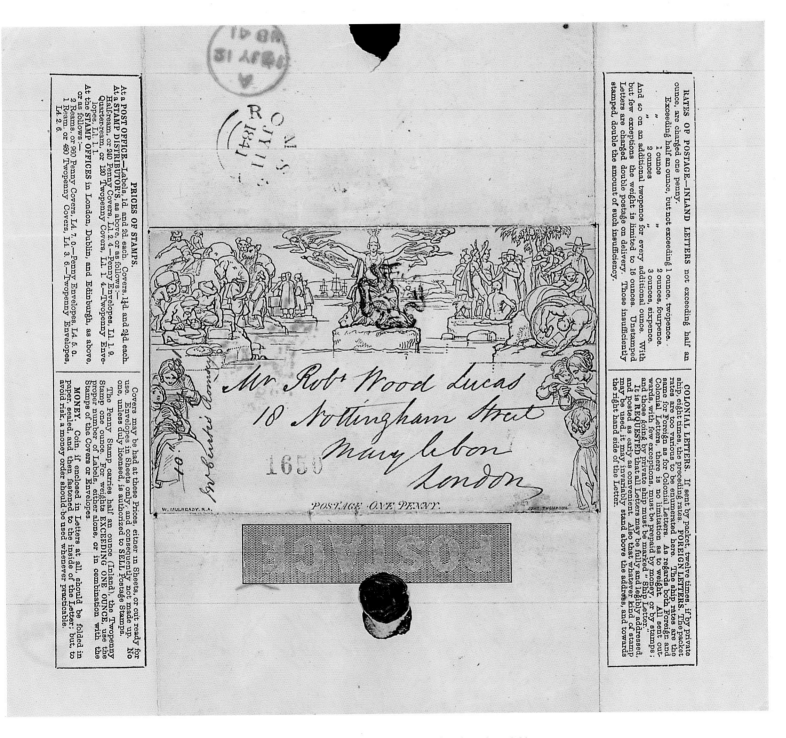

The one-penny wrapper designed by William Mulready and available
for postal use from 6 May 1840. Both ready-made envelopes and wrappers for
folding were put on sale by the Post Office.

The embossed one-penny pink envelope replaced the unpopular Mulready stationery; it remained in use virtually unchanged for over 60 years.

Henrich von Stephan (1831–97), who originally had the idea of using cards as a quick and cheap method of communication, was commemorated on this postcard from Germany on the 1931 centenary of his birth.

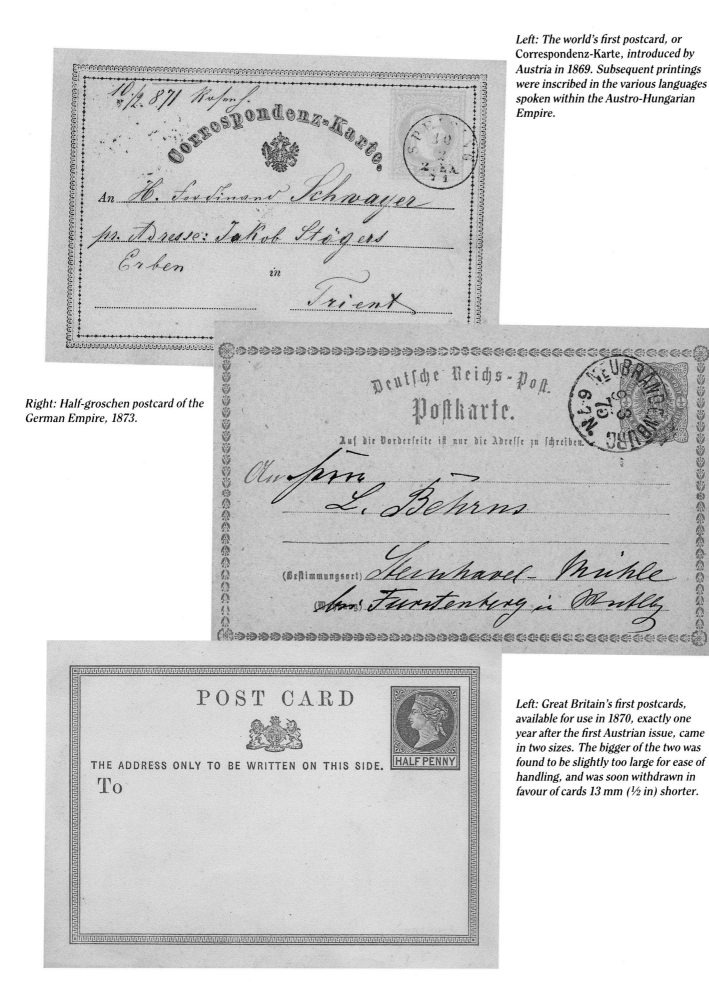

Left: The world's first postcard, or Correspondenz-Karte, introduced by Austria in 1869. Subsequent printings were inscribed in the various languages spoken within the Austro-Hungarian Empire.

Right: Half-groschen postcard of the German Empire, 1873.

Left: Great Britain's first postcards, available for use in 1870, exactly one year after the first Austrian issue, came in two sizes. The bigger of the two was found to be slightly too large for ease of handling, and was soon withdrawn in favour of cards 13 mm (½ in) shorter.

issued to the public today in London for the first time. Great bustle at the stamp office, wrote Hill on that date'). The envelopes were designed by Sir William Mulready; they depicted a central figure of Britannia with attendant lion, sending out winged messengers to peoples of foreign lands, children, and the sick. They were available in two denominations, one penny and two pence, and were intended for use from 6 May 1840, the same day as the new postage stamps. Although a plain pre-paid envelope had been available to Members of Parliament from 16 January (some four months earlier), the Mulready-designed envelopes were the first items of prepaid postal stationery sold to the general public, and as such can be considered as direct forebears of the first official postcards.

The Mulready envelopes did not receive much critical acclaim, however, and a number of caricatures were soon drawn and printed, each lampooning the features of the original. The first of these caricatures appeared within a few weeks, though being unofficial items they were not valid for postage in their own right and had to have a penny stamp attached before posting. Due to its unpopularity Mulready's work was soon withdrawn and replaced by plain envelopes that bore, in the top right-hand corner, an embossed portrait head of Queen Victoria within an oval frame. Embossed stamps had already been suggested when the question of designing the first postage stamps was raised, and now Rowland Hill made use of the idea. A one-penny envelope embossed in pink was put on sale in January 1841, and a two-penny envelope in blue was available from April, each replacing the respective Mulready designs.

Despite the demise of Mulready's offering, his envelopes are remembered as the first to travel through the post bearing decorative pictorial printing on the outside, and therefore paving the way for the many illustrated envelopes that were to follow.

There had in fact been earlier attempts to establish a type of official postal stationery. In Sardinia in 1818, *Carta Postale Bollata* (stamped postal sheets) were sold at state post offices, each letter sheet being impressed with a stamp depicting a horn-blowing horseman, which signified that a tax had been paid

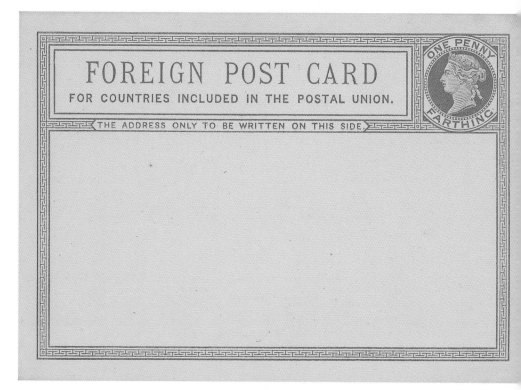

The 'Foreign Post Card' was introduced in 1875, as a result of a General Postal Union agreement stating new postal rates for mail between its member countries.

The public was given the choice between cheaper, thin cards or more expensive stouter ones for its messages.

Left: The first Russian postcard was issued in 1872. This example shortly followed, and was used in 1873.

ОТКРЫТОЕ ПИСЬМО

ИНОГОРОДНОЕ.

Мѣсто для адреса.

St. Petersburg

1. Это письмо можетъ быть опущено въ почтовый ящикъ и отправлено во всѣ почтовыя мѣста Имперіи.
2. На этой сторонѣ кромѣ адреса не дозволяется ничего другаго писать.

Экспед. Заготовл. Государств. Бумагъ.

Right: A bilingual Universal Postal Union card; this one is from the United States.

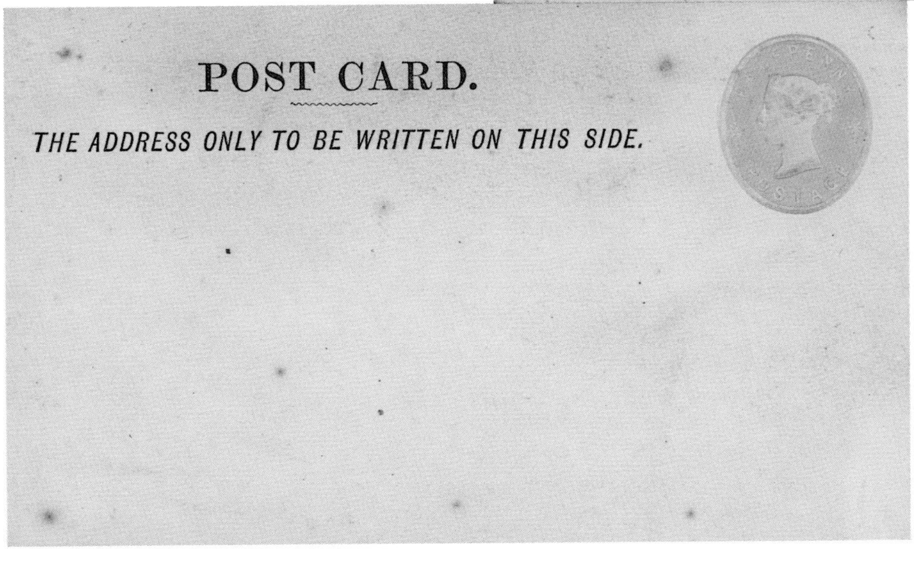

UNIVERSAL POSTAL UNION
(Union Postale Universelle)

UNITED STATES OF AMERICA
(États-Unis d'Amérique)

WRITE ONLY THE ADDRESS ON THIS SIDE

POSTAL CARD

POST CARD.

THE ADDRESS ONLY TO BE WRITTEN ON THIS SIDE.

Left: A privately printed British card embossed with a halfpenny stamp. Stricter regulations concerning the printing and use of private cards in Great Britain and the U.S.A. allowed Continental publishers to gain a head start in issuing decorative, pictorial cards. Picture cards were not permitted in Britain until 1894, by which time publishers elsewhere in Europe were already issuing them as tourist souvenirs.

A German 'Pneumatic Post' card or Rohrpost-Karte, *specially issued for transmission in the pneumatic postal system. Similar methods of mail transportation were also popular in France and Austria.*

on that sheet. In New South Wales, Australia, in 1838, sheets carrying the seal of the colony were sold to the public, and signified prepayments of postage locally. However, such sheets proved unpopular, and it was not until the British penny pink envelope of January 1841 was introduced that an item of postal stationery first attained widespread public acceptance and use. In fact the penny pink envelope turned out to be so popular that it remained in circulation, virtually unaltered, for approximately 61 years.

Now that a cheap postal system had been established (and with it the use of postage stamps and postal stationery), and such a system proved to be working efficiently, the idea naturally spread across the globe. Prepaid stationery was issued in Russia and Finland in 1845, and in several German states shortly after. Later, the United States would have the honour of issuing the first commemorative postal stationery, for the Philadelphia Centennial Exposition of 1876. However, the main action post-1840 shifted away from Britain and to Germany and Austria, where significant developments in terms of postcard his-

tory were made by two gentlemen, Dr Heinrich von Stephan and Dr Emanuel Herrmann, both of whom are recognized as originators of the idea of a 'card post'.

Dr Heinrich von Stephan (1831-97), a German postal official, is credited as being the first person to officially raise the question of an alternative form of postal communication, which was very similar in idea to the postcard in its present form. He realized that letter-writing was a long-winded affair: it was necessary to purchase separate writing paper, envelopes, and stamps, and the contents of the letter were subject to certain pro forma pleasantries (formal greetings, enquiries after health, etc), which meant that a short, quick note was almost impossible. As a solution for those who required it, von Stephan suggested the introduction of a stiff form, of envelope size, which could be directly written on and posted without the need to be enclosed in an envelope. Its nature would preclude the need for formalities in writing, and it would bear a pre-printed postage stamp making it ready for sending. In fact, it was intended that the postal charge would be the only cost to the buyer, ie the card itself was free.

This last fact was to prove a sticking point: the authorities worried that money would be lost as a result of implementing von Stephan's idea and also that because of the number of separate stamp-issuing states operating in the country—during the 1850s and 1860s a number of the German states had their own postal administrations, with each issuing its own stamps—the scheme would be difficult to carry out. In addition to the states, there were the Austrian Counts of Thurn und Taxis, who operated a postal monopoly in those districts without their own administrations. Eventually then, after careful consideration, von Stephan's idea was rejected as being too complicated and costly to carry out. He was not forgotten however: when several of the states (Brunswick, Hamburg, Oldenburg, Lubeck, Bremen, Saxony, and Prussia) joined together to form the North German Confederation (which started issuing its own stamps on 1 January 1868), von Stephan was shortly thereafter appointed its postal director; later, as the Prussian Postmaster General, he was to put forward the proposals that led to the formation of the General Postal Union in 1874.

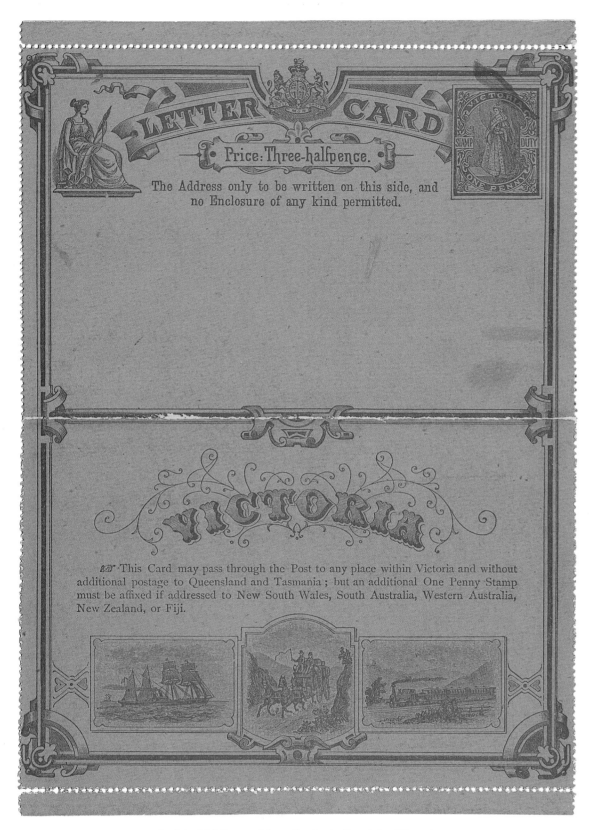

A pictorial letter card from the Australian state of Victoria.

Meanwhile, in Vienna, Austria, in January 1869, Dr Emanuel Herrmann (1839-1902) published an analysis of his country's postal system, concluding that savings could be made by introducing a card the approximate size of an envelope, but specially intended for only a brief message and postable without need of an envelope—all at a cost of about half the standard postage rate. Herrmann's arguments and proposals were very similar to those that von Stephan had put forward, although it was not known if he was aware of the earlier German scheme. The difference was that this time the postal authorities of the Austro-Hungarian Empire decided to act upon the idea, and within the fairly short time of nine months Austria-Hungary had put into practice Herrmann's suggestions.

The momentous day when the world's first postcards became available for use in Austria-Hungary was 1 October 1869. The *Correspondenz-Karte,* as the first Austrian issue was called, came on thin card of a light brown colour. A two-kreuzer stamp was imprinted in the top right-hand corner, and there was also space for the address to be written on the front. A framework, or border, ran around just inside the edges, and the message was intended to be written on the reverse. Fairly unprepossessing by later picture-postcard standards, a certain sense of history nonetheless imbues examples of these first issues, which without doubt represent an important step in the development of postal communication. It would probably be fair to say that the majority of picture postcard collectors do not fully recognize the importance of these plain-looking pieces of card. But the early postal stationery issues, one side of which was left entirely blank for the message, are worthy of a place in any picture-postcard collection, because without them the picture postcard as we know it today would never have evolved.

Although initially intended only for use within the Austro-Hungarian Empire, this new form of postal correspondence immediately proved to be immensely popular. Several million were posted within the first year, and this success led other nations to look at the possibilities of issuing their own postal cards. Somewhat ironically, it was the North German Confederation—which could have been

This Swiss card celebrates 25 years of the Universal Postal Union, whose first meeting had been in Switzerland in 1875.

the actual originator of the card had it accepted the proposals of Heinrich von Stephan—that was the next nation to produce postcards, along with several of the non-affiliated German states (including Wurttemburg and Baden). This was in July 1870, the Germans having given themselves enough time to monitor the postcard's popularity and success since Austria's issue nine months earlier. Again, large sales showed that the public liked these new correspondence cards; indeed, even today examples of these first Austrian and German cards are not too difficult to find due to the great quantities produced and sent through the post in those early days.

The realization that a 'card post' was a viable proposition now began to spread throughout the postal authorities of many other countries, although initially issues were confined to Western Europe. By mid-1871 Great Britain, Switzerland, Luxembourg, Belgium, the Netherlands, and Denmark were all producing their own issues—with the same basic format as the Austrian cards though with differences in dimension.

The first British postcards went on sale on 1 October 1870. Measuring approximately 111 × 90 mm (4⅜ × 3½ in), they were printed on lilac and bore an imprinted halfpenny stamp. However, bearing in mind the small size of envelopes then generally in use, the postcards were soon found to be just a

little too large to be comfortably handled by the postmen of the day, so a second issue 13 mm (½ in) shorter at 121 × 75 mm (4¾ × 3 in), which did not stick out of the postmen's bundle, replaced the original card. Large sections of the British public proved to be no different from their Austrian and German counterparts and bought the cards by the million: some 76 million, in fact, were used during the first year. There is even alleged to have been some dissatisfaction among the postmen of the day, undoubtedly weighed down during their deliveries (as they would have the public believe) by this large increase in the amount of mail to be carried.

However, not all sections of the public welcomed the postcard. Many objections were raised in connection with the open nature of the messages they carried. Those in opposition felt that having the contents of the correspondence visible for all to see made the cards liable to abusive or potentially damaging usage. Offensive messages could be conveyed straight into the Victorian household, unshielded from prying eyes, and tradesmen could claim payment for accounts that did not necessarily exist from persons too afraid of having their reputations damaged by such open requests to make a fuss. Indeed, several cases of libel did find their way into the law courts. Such isolated incidents aside, the introduction of a postcard had proved to be a great success in those countries that had tried it, paving the way for things to come.

The first non-European country to issue a postcard was Canada, in June 1871, after which time significant steps were taken on a worldwide scale. By the end of 1874 countries issuing cards included France, Romania, Russia, most of Scandinavia, Spain, Japan, Italy, Chile, and the United States. It is interesting to note that the latter country did not jump on the bandwagon until May 1873, despite having given some consideration to the issue of a postal card three years earlier. The American postal authorities chose cards of approximately 130 × 75 mm (5⅛ × 3 in) in size, printed in brown, at an all-inclusive price of one cent. By this time success was almost guaranteed: the public bought them at a rate of over two million per week nationwide.

At this point it is worth mentioning an early unofficial (ie, non-government issue) postal card that predated the official versions, and played a part in American postcard history besides. Since 1861 it had been quite acceptable in the United States to send any piece of card through the mail as long as it conformed to postal regulations,' that is, was properly addressed and had the correct value stamp attached. A copyright on a postal card for such use was obtained by a certain John Charlton, and transferred to H. Lipman, the latter producing two issues of his 'Lipman's Postal Card', similar in appearance and function to the later official postcards. Although the printing of this card predates even the first Austrian correspondence card, the earliest known used example is dated a year or so after those first Austrian issues travelled through the post. The importance of Lipman's cards is that they were the first to be known as 'postal cards', and, although not an official issue themselves, they were the first to be sanctioned by a postal authority.

Regarding the early government-issued postcards, it should be added that initially they were intended only to be addressed within the country of origin. To try to send a card abroad, even if an additional stamp was affixed to pay the extra postage, would usually result in its return by the Post Office.

It was not until a few years later, in September 1875, that the General Postal Union was formed, at a conference in Berne, Switzerland, attended by delegates from 22 countries (the General Postal Union became the Universal Postal Union at a second conference in Paris four years later, at which 38 countries were represented). One of the agreements reached at the G.P.U. was a fixed rate of postage for all mail sent from one country to another within the Union. This resulted in new cards being issued by several postal authorities, which were specially intended for foreign use and bore imprinted stamps at the new foreign rates. For example, Great

North German Confederation Correspondenz-Karte, *1870. These did not have stamps imprinted upon them; a standard postage stamp had to be affixed before use.*

Bavarian two-kreuzer card, 1873.

Britain issued a 'Foreign Post Card' (sub-headed 'For Countries included in the Postal Union') at a cost of one penny-farthing, and the German Empire, plus Bavaria and Wurttemburg, a ten-pfennig *Postkarte aus Deutschland* in 1878. Such cards were required, as were all foreign postcards, to be titled bilingually, in the native language and in French, according to regulations introduced by the Union that year.

So by the 1870s the postal stationery postcard was establishing itself around the world as a means of communication that was quick, easy to use, and cheap to send. Occasionally variations on the theme were employed. In 1872 the German Empire and Bavaria issued the first reply cards. Basically, a reply card comprised two cards joined together along one edge, each imprinted with a stamp. The sender would write his message on the top of the card and mail the whole thing, and the recipient would pen his reply on the lower card and send it back, postpaid. Another novelty introduced in France, Germany, and Austria in the mid-1870s was special stationery for transmission in the pneumatic postal systems of those countries.

The pneumatic system—by which containers could be propelled along underground tubes by creating a vacuum ahead of, and increased air pressure behind, the container—was initially tried in Britain in 1826. Such a system was used to convey mailbags in London between 1863 and 1873, and then abandoned. On the Continent, however, it proved more successful, resulting in the issue of the French *Carte Pneumatique* and the German *Rohrpostkarte,* both of which stayed in circulation for many years.

The 1880s saw the introduction of the letter card, which came in the form of a longish sheet of paper with two or three folds across it, the larger space allowing a fuller message to be written. The letter card would then be folded to the size of an envelope, sealed, and, as it bore an imprinted stamp, be ready for posting. Belgium was the first country to issue letter cards, in 1882.

Although very important in their own right, early official cards offered by postal authorities around the globe were plain, functional items. It was only as a result of private enterprise that the first picture-bearing cards started to appear.

ADVERTISEMENTS AND SOUVENIRS: PICTURES IN THE POST

Postcards bearing some form of decoration were the natural successors of the early postal stationery cards. They were partly the result of man's innate desire to adorn and embellish anything that appears plain and ordinary, and partly—perhaps mostly—the result of a need to advertise and make money.

The history of pictorial printing goes back to a time well before the first postcards were envisioned, and although

perhaps these images comprise a field more for the printed ephemera specialist, there are several types of decoratively printed items that could be said to be the forebears of—and therefore an influence on—the first picture postcards. During the second half of the eighteenth century trade cards and tradesman's billheads evolved into very decorative items bearing high-quality engravings.

The 'trade card', as it is now known, originated during the seventeenth cen-

tury as a piece of paper onto which a tradesman's name was engraved. Used for publicity purposes, or for writing out a customer's bill, these cards soon began to carry small pictures that represented the tradesman's line of business (a coach and horses for a stagecoach operator and a boot for a shoemaker, for example), and also included his address and how to get there. The ornate lettering and pictorial vignettes found on these cards were intended to convey the impression

Above: London watchmaker's descriptive trade card bearing pictorial engraving.

Above: Charming colour lithographed sheet-music cover depicting a postman of the mid-Victorian era. Postal-related items such as this are very collectable in themselves.

I'LL SPEAK OF THEE.

—

I'll speak of thee and love thee too,
Fondly and with affection true,
Pure as yon sky's celestial blue,
　　　　　My love shall be.

In sunshine, and tho' clouds may
　　　lower,
In mirth and sorrow's saddening
　　　hour,
While memory lives and life has
　　power,　　　　I'll love thee.

By the middle of Queen Victoria's reign, Valentine cards had already evolved into ornate, decorative items.

of quality and elegance, in order to attract the custom of the upper classes (the lower classes were unlikely to be able to afford the products or services advertised). When customers' bills and company writing paper later evolved as items separate from the trade card, they were headed by the same printed pictures and ornate script.

At about this time, too, visiting cards tended to be highly ornamental. The better-off would have ornate cards carrying their name or perhaps with a design that reflected the bearer's occupation. Alternatively, pictorial cards could be bought that had a space in the design on which the bearer could write his or her name in ink.

During the nineteenth century many printed items carried some form of pictorial decoration—sheet music, writing paper, and broadsides included. Menu cards from the 1840s through the 1860s would have elaborately gilded or embossed

A selection of mid- to late Victorian Christmas cards. Postcards, too, were soon to become as decorative and colourful.

borders, and, perhaps as a predecessor to the holiday-view postcard, booklets containing engraved views of popular resorts were produced by local publishers for sale to visitors.

With the advent of penny postage and the publishing of Mulready's envelope in 1840, the use of pictorially printed envelopes became more widespread. Several publishers issued their own envelopes, or sets of envelopes, the designs of which caricatured that of Mulready's. Of particular note are those published by Fores of Piccadilly and by William Spooner. In the same month that the official envelope appeared, Fores published a design by John Leech with political overtones, in which, along with postal messengers chivying along their underweight mules, Britannia is depicted looking rather the worse for drink. Later in the year Fores also produced a series of ten envelopes, each of which had a particular theme including dancing, hunting, racing, the military, and coaching. These were clearly drawn in a gently amusing manner, something which could *not* be said of the series produced by Spooner, whose envelopes were hard-hitting and disrespectful of the postal system and the monarchy.

Pictorial envelopes soon were being issued for many reasons—politics, romance, and advertising among them. Some series were produced simply with decorative views upon them, whereas the American Civil War saw the flourishing of the patriotic envelope. London's Great Exhibition, held in 1851 in the Crystal Palace, Hyde Park, saw the production of several commemorative envelopes to mark the event. On the executive committee of the Exhibition was Henry (later Sir Henry) Cole (1808-82), who had been the assistant to Rowland Hill in 1840 and had played a large part in the production of the Mulready envelope (he even sketched some preliminary designs for it).

Three years later, in 1843 (the year Dickens' *A Christmas Carol* was published), Cole was responsible for publishing another of the picture postcard's forerunners: the first Christmas card. The card was designed for Cole by John Calcott Horsley, was printed by lithography, and was hand-coloured. About the same size as the first postcards, it depicted an affluent Victorian family enjoying their Christmas dinner and toasting the onlooker with glasses of wine. On either side were small vignettes

Above: Carte-de-visite photographs depicting famous people, views, and works of art became very popular during the 1860s. This example is of the composer Mozart.

Below: Following the Mulready stationery, publishers were quick to see the commercial potential of pictorially printed envelopes. This one was published during the campaign for an Ocean Penny Postage in the early 1860s.

*Two very rare early pictorial cards.
Left: A vignette view of the 1881 Trade and Industry Exhibition at Halle in Germany. A similar card, produced for an exhibition at Nuremburg in 1882, was once believed to be the world's first official pictorial postcard.*

Right: A 1904 postcard which depicts a facsimile of a French card produced in 1870 as a souvenir of the Franco–Prussian War.

showing the less fortunate, and below were the words 'A Merry Christmas and a Happy New Year to You'. In small print at the bottom was printed 'Published at Summerly's Home Treasury Office, Old Bond Street, London'. The reverse of the card was blank. A thousand of these cards were printed, of which very few remain today; an example actually addressed to Henry Cole came up for auction in November 1987 and fetched £2,000. Besides playing a large part in the introduction of postage stamps and Christmas cards, both taken for granted today, Cole went on to do other fine work, including establishing and becoming the first director of London's Victoria and Albert Museum.

The next decade saw the introduction of the carte-de-visite photograph, a phenomenon that experienced considerable success in the 1860s. These small photographs were produced en masse and, like the later postcards, depicted famous people, views, works of art, and many other popular subjects of the day, some in colour. Soon family portraits were being taken by local photographers, and many households possessed a family photograph album in which to display them.

In America regulations allowed pieces of card to be sent through the mail if correctly addressed and stamped, and in Continental Europe, too, many examples of the early postal usage of advertising

cards and trade cards have been recorded. Usually of approximate envelope size, they would carry publicity for the sender's business and might also incorporate some form of pictorial decoration in the message. However, no mention of the term 'postcard', or its equivalent, would appear on them, and a stamp of the value of the normal letter rate had to be attached. Therefore, as they were not eligible to be posted at a reduced (postcard) rate, such items cannot be truly defined as 'postcards' in the now accepted sense of the word. What they did do was to make people realize, when the first official cards came out, that here was a good opportunity to achieve some desired publicity, this time without having to affix a stamp of the full letter rate.

Initially, the postal authorities of each country restricted the use of postcards to their own official issues; it was not for a few years that members of the public were allowed to print their own. Therefore, anyone desiring to print an advertisement onto a card had to use one that had been bought from a post office. In Britain the Post Office facilitated this by supplying sheets of cards that could be printed upon, individually separated, and posted in the normal way. Only large quantities of these sheets would be supplied, so consequently the small businessman who would have liked to print a few dozen cards for his own use could not afford to take part. One such advertisement upon a post office card was used by the Royal Polytechnic Institution in London, printed to publicize forthcoming entertainments within its walls and sent out to its patrons. Lever Brothers also printed a Sunlight Soap advertisement, in the form of lettering and a small pictorial vignette, along the top of the back of a post office card. Christmas 1870 saw the printing of various festive greetings, with a festive verse surrounded by holly and mistletoe taking up all of the back of a card. This idea was also adopted in the United States a few years later, with examples bearing pictorial decoration and the words 'Merry Christmas and a Happy New Year 1874' diagonally across the centre of the back.

Shortly after the introduction of the official postcard, a number of postal authorities made a concession that accelerated the arrival of the pictorial card. This was to allow members of the public to manufacture and print their own cards, so there were no longer restrictions saying that only the official issues could be printed upon. The use of private cards was introduced in Great Britain in June 1872 and in Germany one month later, although there were still many rules and regulations as to what would be acceptable for transmission through the post. Privately manufactured cards had to be the same size as the official ones and of a certain thickness, and there had to be a space left in the top right-hand corner in which the Post Office could imprint the official stamp (the public was still not allowed to affix an ordinary stamp to these cards if they were to be sent at the special postcard rate; for this

Standard postal stationery card of 1890 bearing two of the special commemorative postmarks in use at the Guildhall Exhibition held that year. The postmarks could be obtained by the payment of a small fee.

they still had to be taken to the Revenue Office for stamping).

In some countries more use was made of this concession than in others. The businessmen of Germany, for example, issued cards with small vignette views printed on them—not, however, on the reverse, but on the same side as the address and stamp, usually in the top left-hand corner. These views, printed in one colour, would usually publicize a particular hotel and depict it in its picturesque mountain setting; these were the precursors of today's view postcards. Cards bearing small illustrations are also believed to have been made available to the troops involved in the Franco-Prussian War of 1870, and so it seems that mainland Europe was the first area to take the initiative in the matter of the pictorial decoration of cards. The stricter regulation governing their use in Great Britain and the United States played a large part in the subsequent later development of these two countries when it came to pictorial postcard publishing.

Over the next couple of decades the picture-view postcard started to establish itself, mainly in mainland Europe. Vignettes of popular towns, holiday resorts, castles, and restaurants proliferated, and now these images were on the reverse (non-address) side. In Britain cards with advertisements were still being produced, whereas in Germany, Austria, and Switz-

erland views were beginning to appear in colour and were taking up more and more space, leaving only a small area on which to write a message. This meant that postcards were now being sent as decorative items in their own right, and any communications they carried often took second place to the pictures they bore. Of course, although the craze for picture cards was now gathering pace, the numbers being issued were still only a very small fraction of the great quantities that were to appear ten to fifteen years later; and as many were thrown away (because the collecting of them had not yet become established as a pastime), these early issues did not survive in large numbers and can therefore be difficult to find today.

Since the Great Exhibition of 1851 held at the Crystal Palace, such fairs had become very popular with the Victorian public, and some of the very first commemorative postcards were issued in conjunction with them. Just as pictorial envelopes had been sold as souvenirs at the 1851 exhibition, so postcards were similarly offered at exhibitions elsewhere in Europe during the 1880s and 1890s. One of the first was at the Nuremberg Exhibition of 1882, where an official commemorative card was published bearing a small vignette view on the address side, placed centrally rather than in the corner. Later during the same

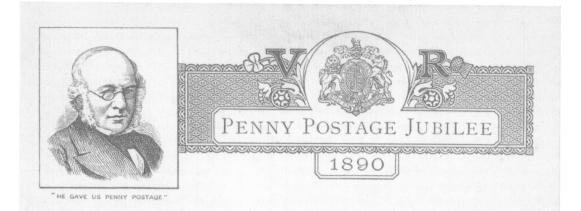

Penny Postage Jubilee envelope and card sold at the South Kensington Exhibition, July 1890.

decade, cards were sold at events held in other European cities such as Brussels and Amsterdam, but it was not until the Paris Exposition of 1889 that these pictorial souvenirs really made a hit with the public. Various designs showing the brand-new Eiffel Tower found great favour with the many who attended the exhibition, and from then on it seemed that every such national and international event had its own souvenir cards, be they officially issued or privately produced.

The year 1890 saw the 50th anniversary of the introduction of penny postage in London. Two events took place to celebrate this jubilee, each accompanied by an official souvenir card. However, neither could correctly be called a true postcard. The first, sold at an exhibition in the Guildhall in May that year, did not actually bear a view, but the address side carried an illustration of the arms of the City of London and the Royal Monogram, as well as an imprinted penny stamp, all in red. A total of ten thousand were printed, all of which sold quickly on the first day (16 May). Many were posted at the exhibition site and therefore were stamped with the special commemorative postmark in use there;

after they had all been sold (and up until the end of the event, 19 May), it was still possible to post an ordinary post office card on the site in order to get the special hand-stamp on it. Although generally accepted as a true postcard, this is not strictly the case, as its size exceeded that of the official postal cards then in use. Therefore, because its dimensions were greater than the maximum allowed for postal transmission at the reduced halfpenny rate, it had to go at the normal letter rate; hence the imprinted one-penny stamp.

The second card to commemorate the jubilee was issued in conjunction with an event at the South Kensington Museum in July 1890. This time an envelope was printed, in blue, headed 'Post Office Jubilee of Uniform Penny Postage', depicting postmen of 1840 and 1890, a mail coach of 1790 ('8 miles an hour') and a mail train of 1890 ('48 miles an hour'). The card came in the form of an insert, bore a portrait of Rowland Hill, and was intended to be written on and posted *within* the envelope. The card itself did not have an imprinted stamp upon it and was not valid for postal transmission on its own. However, this did not stop some people from using

it as a postcard and posting it either unstamped or with a stamp affixed. Far larger numbers of this issue were sold than the Guildhall card, and it is still fairly common today. Also of note, and in the tradition of the Mulready envelope 50 years earlier, a caricature was produced on which, among other things, the original heading, 'Post Office Jubilee', was changed to 'Post Office Jumble'.

In the year 1891 a postcard depicting the Eddystone Lighthouse was issued, in connection with the Royal Naval Exhibition that was held on the grounds of Chelsea Hospital. This time the small illustration appeared on the reverse of the card, but still left plenty of room for the message. Commemorative postmarks were again in use, and can be found stamped in either blue or violet on cards posted from the exhibition site. Similar, but slightly more decorative, postcards were produced for the 1893 Gardening and Forestry Exhibition at Earls Court; it would appear that fewer of these were sold, as they are slightly scarcer today than their 1891 counterparts.

Another exhibition that took place in 1893 marked a milestone in American postcard production. As in Great Britain,

French postcard with advertising vignette of the Terminus Hotel, restrictive postal regulations had resulted in America's lagging behind in the publishing of pictorial cards. The World's Columbian Exposition in Chicago saw the first official pictorial cards offered for sale in that country. Charles W. Goldsmith, the franchise holder, produced a set of ten designs, each in full colour and printed by the American Lithographic Company using the chromolithographic process. Larger than the normal official postal cards of the time,

each depicted a vignette view of one of the particular buildings constructed within the Exposition. There were initially ten different cards, sold by vending machines on the grounds, or alternatively the full set could be purchased together, within a wrapper. A subsequent printing of this series saw new designs being substituted for a couple of the original ones, and, as the event ran from 1 May for a full six months, there was plenty of time for privately printed unofficial

illustrated cards to be produced and find their way onto the market.

Although not of any great rarity, the official Columbian Exposition cards do mark a significant step in American picture-postcard publishing; a complete set of the original ten would be a very desirable item to have. Indeed, all of these early pictorial cards are becoming more and more sought-after, as their importance within the field of postal history becomes better appreciated.

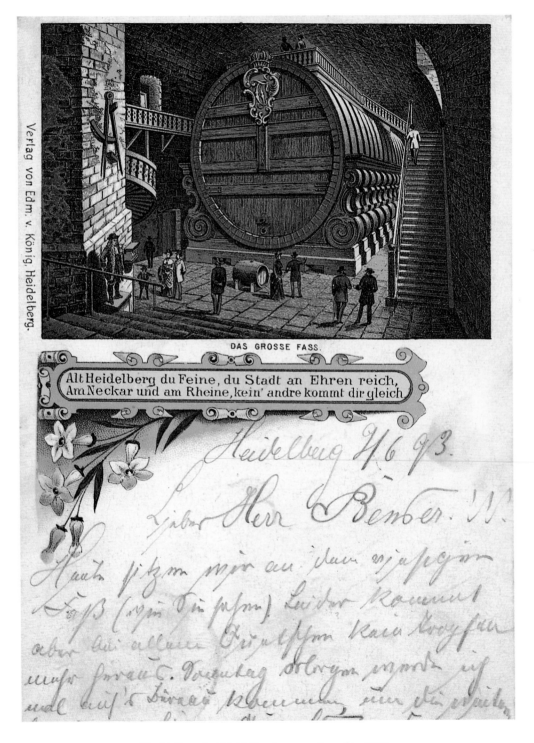

The big barrel at Heidelberg on a card used in 1893.

The 50th anniversary of the Swiss postal service was commemorated by this official card in 1893. Issued as a limited edition it was valid for use for a period of only six months before being withdrawn.

In 1893 the first commercially produced pictorial cards appeared in the United States, published to commemorate the World's Columbian Exposition held in Chicago. Printed by the American Lithographic Company of New York, a set of ten chromolithographic souvenir views was initially issued, of which this is design No. 2.

THE POSTCARD COMES OF AGE

By the early 1890s postcards bearing some kind of picture or view were becoming more readily available on the Continent, and this head start was to prove advantageous to German printers when the sending and collecting of cards became a worldwide craze a few years later.

As well as being issued in conjunction with exhibitions, cards commemorating other events or marking particular anniversaries were now beginning to appear. The marriage or death of certain members of the German monarchy had been remembered in this way, as had the 50th anniversary of the Swiss Postal Service in 1893. The following year a particularly important card was issued to commemorate a particularly notable event—the 25th anniversary of the introduction of the postcard itself. Not surprisingly issued in Austria, it honoured Dr Emanuel Herrmann, depicting his head-and-shoulders portrait within a fancy framework, with the words *Jubiläums Karte* and brief details of the reason for its issue to the right of the portrait. A scarce card in its own right, such early 'postcards about postcards' are additionally desirable with many collectors today. (Interestingly, Germany issued a card in 1905 honouring von Stephan, commemorating the 40th anniversary of his original proposal in 1865 and claiming the postcard idea as his.)

Historic events, exhibitions, and royal visits gradually were being commemorated on the postcards of other European countries, such as Italy, Spain, France, and Russia, and thus helped to spread their popularity to a wider audience. Also, the phenomenon known as the *Gruss aus* postcard was spreading the postal word far and wide: taking the basic view card with its pictorial vignettes of a particular town as a starting point, someone had the simple idea of adding the words *Gruss aus . . .* (literally, 'Greetings from . . .') into the design, followed by the town name, thus immediately creating for the tourist a cheap, decorative souvenir with the bonus of naming the places they were visiting for the benefit of the folks back home. These *Gruss aus* cards are the direct forerunners of today's holiday-view postcards, and they did not take long to catch on in the 1890s. Soon every seaside town and tourist attraction had its own 'Greetings from' card, and the idea quickly spread around the world, with the greeting in the appropriate language (*Souvenir de . . .* in French and *Ricordi de . . .* in Italian, for example).

As an added boost to sales, these early cards, which had been printed in one

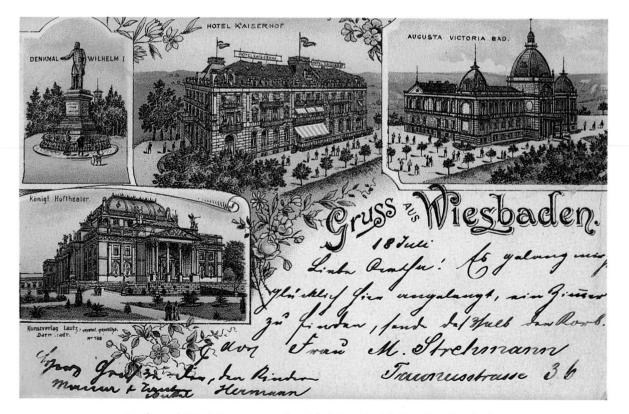

By the early 1890s Gruss aus *cards, with their pictorial view vignettes, had established themselves in Germany, and their popularity quickly spread. This example extends greetings from Wiesbaden.*

'Greetings From Salzburg', a view vignette with chromolithographic decoration.

German card celebrating Bismarck's 80th birthday, in 1895.

Grands Magasins DE LA VILLE DE SAINT-DENIS Nouveautés
Faubg St Denis et Rue de Paradis - PARIS.

Chasseurs d'Afrique 1833
TENUE DE GUERRE

Fine early French military vignette with advertising overprint.

colour, were now being supplemented by beautiful high-quality colour examples printed by a process called chromolithography, by which many different deep, vivid colours could be applied to make a fine, detailed picture. More and more people were now travelling abroad—it no longer was a pastime exclusively for the wealthy—so such cards found ready buyers. Also, the cards' attractiveness made their recipients at home loath to throw them away, hence the souvenir postcard album was born.

Most of this early development in picture postcards was taking place on the Continent, with Great Britain and the United States lagging behind. Post Office regulations remained the basic stumbling block, for they still severely restricted what could and could not be sent through the post. It was not permissible to mail a privately printed card bearing an adhesive stamp: only the official issues with imprinted stamps could be used. So while the German and Austrian publishers were producing and selling to the public what the public wanted, ie, decorative, colourful postcards, no such activity was going on in Britain and America.

In Britain, campaigns were waged against the postal authorities in an attempt to effect changes that would bring

the regulations concerning postcards more into line with their European counterparts. A Member of Parliament, John Henniker Heaton, was at the forefront of these exchanges, but since the Post Office was making a reasonable amount of money from the sale of official cards, the authorities were none too keen to acquiesce to his proposals. However, the tide of public opinion could not be ignored forever, reinforced as it was by the fine examples of pictorial cards that were coming from mainland Europe, and so, from 1 September 1894, privately printed cards onto which a halfpenny stamp could be affixed were eventually allowed. This made the printing of decorative cards commercially viable, and certain publishing companies were quick to produce series with pictorial view vignettes on them. George Stewart & Co's set bearing small views of Edinburgh, and Beeching's series of vignettes of typical London scenes, were among the first to appear, and over the next few years other publishers entered the market with local-view vignettes of towns up and down the country. Yet a sudden proliferation of these pictures in the post did not just happen overnight, and British pictorial cards postally used before 1897 are scarce.

One of the contributing factors as to

why Continental issues were still superior to British ones was that of card size. Although they allowed privately published cards to be used from September 1894, the British postal authorities still imposed certain restrictions, one being that any private card should be as nearly as possible the same size as the official ones. This was considerably smaller than the size of their European counterparts and meant that the foreign issues could be anything up to 36 per cent larger in area than home-produced examples and, of course, the more room there was to play with, the more attractive the pictures could be. In January the following year, the Post Office officially introduced a new size card, squarer in shape, which came to be known, somewhat mysteriously, as the 'court card'. Court cards remained in use for several years, but still only measured approximately 115 × 90 mm (4½ × 3½ in), a full 25 mm (1 in) shorter than those in use abroad.

Toward the end of the century, more and more court cards started to appear; the majority bore printed photographic-view vignettes, although chromolithographic examples could be found. But as the German printers had been producing quality colour cards for some while, they had taken quite a lead in

Early photographic card, sent from Austria in 1897.

Dutch Gruss aus-type card with pretty chromolithographic vignettes. Because messages were not allowed to be written on the reverse, cards on which the correspondent has made use of every inch of available space on the picture side are often found.

this field, and their techniques were superior to and cheaper than anything available elsewhere. For this reason, until printers in other countries caught up, most publishers would design their own cards but have them printed abroad, usually in Saxony or Bavaria. Lack of enterprise was also cited as a reason why British printers lagged behind their German counterparts; only if there was an incentive to produce and sell more postcards would British printers feel the need to compete.

In the United States such a boost to the postcard industry came about in 1898, as from 1 July of that year privately produced cards were allowed to be used. Advertisements had occasionally appeared printed onto official government cards previous to this, but it is effectively from this date that American picture-postcard production, and for that matter, collecting, took off. Many manufacturers immediately went into business, producing postcards that had to be inscribed, according to the regulations, 'Private Mailing Card—Authorized by Act of Congress, 19 May 1898'.

Above: A 'court'-size example advertising the Howard Hotel, London, 25 mm (1 in) shorter than the standard cards in use elsewhere in Europe.

Below: Body builder John Grün, one of the 'Remarkable Men of Luxembourg' from an 1897 series.

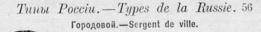

Above: Greetings and advertising overprinted on a Hungarian military card, 1899.

Left: Russian police sergeant, 1899. Note the cryptic message: 'He was much needed here a few evenings ago'.

Meanwhile, in Europe publishers were starting to get more adventurous. Until this time, the great majority of cards had really only depicted views of various kinds, be they seaside resorts, hotels, mountain scenes, famous places of public entertainment, or scenes within exhibitions. Many of these pictures, especially the fine chromolithographic cards of the late 1890s, were painted by artists especially for postcard reproduction, but the artist's name did not appear and was not considered important by either the publisher or the card-buying public.

Around 1897-98, sets of cards started to appear that changed this, for they were issued especially to showcase the work of some of the finest and most popular artists of the day. Here the illustrators were all-important, so their signatures usually appeared within the design; through these the postcard established itself as something to be taken seriously by those who had considered the seaside greetings and comic views too frivolous for their tastes. These early Continental series generally reproduced in postcard form, famous poster or

Cards depicting all forms of animal life have always been published in quantity. Currently most popular are those of animals drawn in human situations or dressed in human clothes, like this German chromolithographic example.

Charming chromolithographic Gruss aus-*type card depicting the Variety Theatre in Prague.*

Cycling is now a popular subject with collectors. This example was published in Belgium in 1898.

'Greetings from Niagara Falls', an American Gruss aus-type card.

51

Comic bathers on a Belgian card, 1900.

magazine illustrations by many of the most talented artists of the period. The numbers printed were usually limited, thus giving the cards an air of exclusivity that they retain to the present day.

One of the first of these series was published in France in 1898. *Editions Cinos* reproduced 35 posters by top-ranking artists, many publicizing famous Parisian places of entertainment. Included in the series were four designs by Alphonse Mucha for roles played by Sarah Bernhardt; Jules Chéret's posters for the Casino de Paris and the Palais de Glace; Eugène Grasset's *Century Magazine,* and a very highly prized Henri de Toulouse-Lautrec design for the Moulin Rouge. Such cards are today regarded as classics of the postcard

world, and their scarcity and desirability means that, when they can be found, they tend to be expensive.

Another French collection, *Les Maîtres de la Carte Postale,* also started in 1898 and was issued over the next couple of years. Published in Paris, a total of 58 cards was issued in six series, each bearing the series number and artist's name, with a few additionally titled. Artists of the day whose work was included in more than one series include, among others, Couturier, Jordic, and Chapront, and several fine pen-and-ink vignettes of country scenes by P. Vibert can be found. In Austria and Germany, too, fine titled collections of cards were being published before the turn of the century, such as the *Jugend* series, totalling 75

cards and including the work of some fine artists in the Jugendstil, or German Art Nouveau, style; and also *Das Grosse Jahrhundert,* a large series different in content to the others mentioned in that each card celebrated a personality internationally recognized in his field—the likes of Mozart, Beethoven, Darwin, Marconi, Tolstoi, and Goethe are among those represented.

A card depicting the Norwegian explorer Fridtjof Nansen, famous for his expedition to the North Pole that set out in 1893, is also found in the *Das Grosse Jahrhundert* series. Heroic deeds such as polar explorations were latched onto by postcard publishers; indeed, most such expeditions of the next several decades were accompanied by a

*reiterated many times on postcards of the late 1890s. These two examples,
both by the same publisher, are typical of their type.*

A Portuguese vignette sent from Mozambique in 1898. Addressed to the War Office in London, it carries a coded message on the reverse.

commemorative issue of postcards. In Nansen's case, a superb rare composite set of four cards was produced, which, when placed together in rectangular formation, made one large picture—with the globe (showing the North Pole) in the centre, and small scenes depicting polar bears, a portrait of Nansen, and his ice-bound ship around the edges; the words *Fridtjof Nansen, Nord Polar-Expedition* surrounded the central globe. In 1898 a series of twelve cards depicting scenes from this expedition was published by Meissner & Buch, a company that would go on to gain international recognition for the quality of the chromo-lithographic postcards it was to produce.

A Belgian Antarctic expedition in 1897 was similarly commemorated by a series of cards, as was the ill-fated attempt to reach the North Pole in a hot-air balloon by a Frenchman, Solomon Andrée, in the same year. A *Gruss aus*-type card showing the balloon setting off from Spitzbergen can be considered one of the earliest aviation postcards; Andrée, however, did not return, although his body and the records he kept were discovered in 1930, an event that saw a few more postcards issued to commemorate him. It also seemed reasonable that, as the ever-popular *Gruss aus* cards were now apparently coming from everywhere, the latest addition was, of course, 'Gruss vom Nordpol'!

Other events to be commemorated

Left and below: Two saucy French turn-of-the-century cards by G. Mouton, depicting the Parisian way of life.

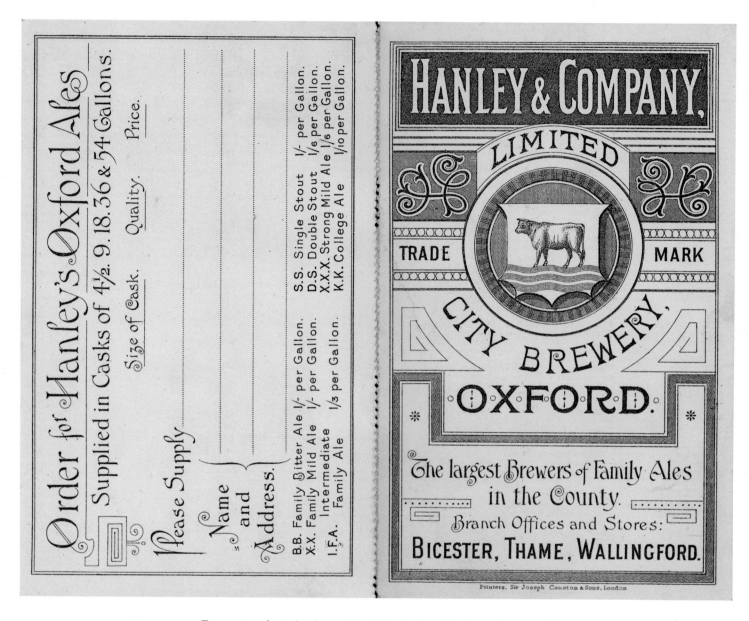

Two-part perforated order card for Hanley's Ales with decorative engraving.

on the picture postcard during the last few years of the century included, in Germany, the visit of Czar Nicholas II and Czarina Alexandra in October 1896, and Kaiser Wilhelm's 100th birthday in March 1897; in Great Britain, the Diamond Jubilee of Queen Victoria (for which various cards were issued in 1897), and in France a certain amount of interest was generated among publishers by the trial of Alfred Dreyfus in 1899. During this time the ever-increasing number of exhibitions taking place in the major cities of Europe still were accompanied by the obligatory souvenir postcards, such as the Transvaal Exhibition in Berlin (1897), the Jubilee Exhibition in Vienna (1898), and the Nice and Venice Exhi-

bitions of 1899, the latter two being of some importance as the subject of both was the picture postcard itself.

As the last few months ticked by toward the year 1900, the number of decorative pictures appearing in the shops was slowly increasing. Yet in Britain there was still something holding back the development of the industry: the question of postcard size continued to rankle the British publishers and public alike. For years now they had seen their European neighbours using the Universal Postal Union-approved larger-dimensioned cards, measuring 140 × 90 mm (5½ × 3½ in), and yet the Post Office was still blocking the introduction of these in Britain, where the court card

(an inch shorter in length) was still the largest available. An 'intermediate' size card was available for a short while that was longer than the court card, but its width (top-to-bottom when looking at the address side) was reduced, so its overall area was no greater. This, therefore, was not the answer.

It was strongly felt that British designers and publishers could only do themselves justice if given the full U.P.U.-sized cards on which to create their miniature works of art; anything smaller would restrict the picture to a cramped vignette tucked away in a corner (as had often been the case in the past). Also, of course, at this time the address and stamp were intended to take up all of one side of the card,

Six cards from the rare 'Editions Cinos' series, published in Paris in 1898.

Official Swiss card marking the inauguration of a commemorative monument to the foundation of the Universal Postal Union.

Most exhibitions seemed to be accompanied by obligatory souvenir postcards; this example is for an event in Düsseldorf, 1902.

and the message had to share the space with the picture on the other side. So if the design was to be a reasonable size on the court cards, where was there going to be room for a few words of greeting? The larger-sized cards were necessary, as surely, it was argued, the average Englishman was entitled to write as much on his postcards as his German and French neighbours, and without having to cramp his handwriting to the extent whereby it could hardly be read.

Mr Henniker Heaton (who had been a thorn in the Post Office's side during the 1894 'privately printed postcard' debate) was again involved, and another chief campaigner of the time was Adolph Tuck. Tuck had succeeded his father, Raphael, as Managing Director of their fine art publishing company, Raphael Tuck & Sons Ltd. Over the previous 30 or so years, the company had gained recognition as being a leader in the field of quality publishing, with its fine range of embossed scraps, greetings cards, calendars, and books. For quite some time Adolph had campaigned to persuade the postal authorities to introduce the larger-size postcards, so that from their newly erected offices in Moorgate, London (they also had premises in New York and Paris), Tuck could bring his firm's excellence to bear on what was for them a new market.

Finally, the Post Office relented and altered the regulations on postcard dimensions. For the first time, cards of the full Universal Postal Union-agreed size were allowed in Great Britain, and the date from which they would be permitted was set at 1 November 1899. It is reasonable to assume that Tuck was given advance warning of this date; certainly, in late August and September the forthcoming change in regulations was publicized in the national press, so other publishing houses must also have known several months beforehand. However, the firm of Raphael Tuck & Sons was first off the mark and its initial issues mark a significant step in postcard history, regarded as they are as being the first full-sized cards to appear in Britain. In the light of the many, many thousands of quality cards that were to subsequently appear with the Tuck trademark, these first few examples gain an additional significance for the postcard collector.

The first Tuck series consisted of twelve cards, each entitled 'The Raphael Tuck

Unusual turn-of-the-century Viennese commemorative card.

& Sons "View" Post Card' and duly numbered. Each depicted a chromo-lithographic view of London and many famous landmarks were included, such as St Pauls Cathedral (No. 2), Westminster Abbey (No. 5), The Houses of Parliament (No. 7), The Bank of England (No. 10), and Trafalgar Square (No. 11). The Tower of London was given the honour of adorning No. 1. Eight of the cards were of a horizontal format and four were vertical, the pictures taking up approximately two-thirds of the available area. With the issue of these, the

Raphael Tuck firm had taken its first real steps into pictorial postcard publishing and looked set to lead the way forward in this field into the new century. Since private-publishing restrictions had been removed in the United States the previous year and cards were already selling well in Europe, it seemed the dawn of the postcard age had begun.

The next few years would tell whether this potential would be realized and whether a simple piece of pictorial card was, in fact, something the public could get excited about.

Above: Raphael Tuck & Sons' 'View Post Card No. 1', the first full-sized card available in Great Britain. The Universal Postal Union allowed postcards 140 × 90 mm (5½ × 3½ in) in dimension to be used, but the British Post Office blocked their use until November 1899. The beauty of the larger designs coming from the Continent played a part in persuading the Post Office to withdraw their objections. Tuck responded to the challenge by issuing 48 of these fine river Thames views on the newly printed, larger-dimensioned cards.

Left: Embossed heraldic card from Belgium, 1900.

German cards to commemorate the new century, one postmarked on the last day of the old (31.12.99), the other on the first day of the new (1.1.00).

PHOTOGRAPHS AND PAINTINGS: VIEWS OF A GOLDEN AGE

Within the first few months of the twentieth century, Raphael Tuck & Sons had produced a number of fine sets of picture postcards using the glorious colours of the chromolithographic technique, some additionally embossed. They were usually sold in packets of six cards to a set, although several series contained twelve cards such as the first series of London views (series No. 1). The second, third, and fourth continued the same theme, making a total of 48 cards, each depicting a vignette view of London or a picturesque scene along the River Thames. Many of these early Tuck cards do not actually bear the series number, only the card's own individual number, thus making some of them difficult to place within a particular set; however, the general public at the time of Victoria's last year as queen would not have been bothered very much with such things as set and series numbers, and many were undoubtedly converted to the joys of picture-postcard sending and collecting as a result of seeing these fine early Tuck specimens.

A further superb collection of cards (among many others) on a view theme was issued by Raphael Tuck the following year: the renowned 'Heraldic' range. Each series depicted landmarks found in the famous towns and cities of Great

Rural Life: The Sower.

Left: 'The Sower' from Raphael Tuck's 'Rural Life' series. The picture postcard captured many such scenes which were soon to be replaced by mechanization.
Below: An original packet in which one of the many sets of cards issued for the Paris Exhibition of 1900 would have been sold. Such packets are usually scarcer than the cards they contained.

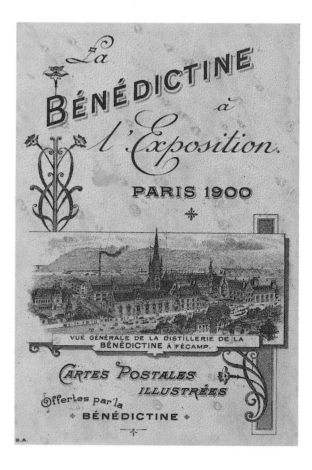

A view vignette card sent from the offices of The Picture Postcard *magazine,
an early publication for those interested in the hobby of collecting cards. The
first issue appeared in July 1900, and the journal was published, with a slight
change of name, until 1907. The example illustrated was written and sent by
E. W. Richardson, the magazine's editor.*

Britain; there was a view in the top right-hand area, together with a coloured, embossed coat-of-arms of the relevant town on the left. The first ten such series showed the attractions of London, Glasgow, Manchester, Liverpool, Dublin, Edinburgh, Birmingham, Belfast, and Bristol, with over three dozen such series issued altogether.

Several cards had been published by Tuck depicting views of the *Exposition Universelle* held in Paris in 1900, the exhibition theme still proving to be popular with the publishers of the day and continuing to be so. This turn-of-the-century event was the biggest yet held, and although souvenir cards had been sold at the Eiffel Tower during the 1889 exhibition in Paris, it was this first great attraction of the twentieth century that really awoke the French to what the

postcard had to offer. The *Palais de l'Electricité* (the fair's main entrance, lit by electricity) and the twenty buildings in the Rue des Nations, each representing a particular country, were depicted on many series of cards from a wide variety of publishers, some of photographic origin and others taken from paintings and drawings specially commissioned. This resulted in one of the most thorough coverages of any event so far depicted on picture postcards, an event that would be forgotten today had it not coincided with the beginnings of this new universal hobby. The same can be said of many of the attractions and events of the Edwardian age, which, despite being important in their own time, are mainly remembered only because the photographers and publishers of that age did such a good and thorough

job of documenting those occasions on the picture postcard.

One of the earlier British companies to establish itself in postcard publication, E. Wrench Ltd, issued an important series of commemorative/view cards in 1901, which were given the name 'Links of Empire'. The first two Links of Empire series commemorated the Foundation of the Commonwealth of Australia and were produced to accompany the Duke and Duchess of Cornwall and York's journey from Portsmouth to Australia and back. Series 1 (ten cards) depicted views on the outward journey, such as Gibraltar, Malta, Port Said, Sydney, and Brisbane, and series 2 (also ten cards), the return via Durban, Cape Town, Montreal, and Newfoundland. What set these cards apart was that it was possible to place an order for the whole series,

Chromolithographic Gruss aus *cards like this were typical of the earlier views issued by publishers for the tourist market.*

An example with embossed coat-of-arms from Raphael Tuck's 'Heraldic' series of 1901.

Another view with embossed arms, this time of German origin.

Elevated R. R. Curve at 110th Street, New York.

Copyright 1905 by the Rotograph Co.

A 183a. West St. looking North, N. Y. City

Printed photographic cards of New York, c1905.

Italian chromolithographic 'regimental' view with vaguely Art Nouveau styling, 1902.

each card to be sent to the purchaser's address from the appropriate port of call and thus bearing the relevant postmark. A similar service was offered for the third Links of Empire series, this one commemorating Captain Scott's Antarctic Expedition on the ship *Discovery*. The set of four, showing Scott, and ship, and his team, could likewise be ordered from the ports of call en route, each additionally having an 'Antarctic Expedition, 1901, S. S. Discovery' cachet stamped upon it. Each purchaser of such a set received, prior to dispatch, a pictorial card from the publishers by way of a receipt for the two shillings that the set cost, some of these acknowledgement cards being signed by Mr Wrench himself.

By 1902 it was clear that the 'Golden Age' of postcards had arrived. Cheaper and better printing techniques were making cards more economical to produce, which resulted in many new postcard-publishing houses being born over the next few years, each trying to make some money out of the new craze. Some would establish themselves by producing quality cards over a long period of time, others found the going tougher and would fold after only a few years in the business. A number of other businesses involved in allied publishing

trades added postcards to their activities, as did those involved in art and photography. Indeed, many of the most sought-after cards today, those important as records of a past way of life, were produced by local photographers who captured on film the rural population at work and play; these cards, made primarily for local sale, could depict scenes and events that the large national publishers could not hope, or did not wish, to cover.

The last major development in the postcard occurred in 1902, and since then the card's basic format has remained unchanged to the present day. This final change in postcard format concerned the back of the card, and on this occasion it was Great Britain rather than mainland Europe that led the way. Initially, when the first plain postal stationery cards were issued, the 'front' referred to the side with the address and stamp on it, the 'back' being the other side, which was blank. Since the development of picture cards, on which an artist-drawn or photographic view had taken over most of the non-address side, this had now become known as the 'front'; therefore, because of the appearance of these first pictures, the address was now the 'back'.

Since the 1880s the picture had been

gradually taking over the whole space available on the front of the postcard. Although there was usually still room left for a message, there was often only enough space for half a dozen words because, of course, the larger the picture, the more attractive it could be. Regulations prohibited correspondence to be written on the address side, so if the sender had a fair bit of news to tell, he or she would be forced to write over the picture, which somewhat spoiled its beauty. Such an occurrence did not seem to matter as much on the *Gruss aus* vignette views, which were designed for such a purpose (indeed a short message on the front often added to their charm). But by 1902 many fine-art cards were being published, in particular the chromolithographs published by Tuck and some superb Art Nouveau cards from various publishers, and it seemed a pity to have to write on the face of these. However, as messages were not allowed to be written on the back, there was no alternative. Indeed, on looking through Edwardian albums, early top-quality cards, when they do turn up, are often found with lines of correspondence written over and detracting from the beauty of the picture.

The proposals put forward early in

Southsea. The Common from Clarence Pier.

Typical coloured view of a seaside town. Although 'divided-back' cards were available in 1902, 'undivided backs', with a small space for a few words on the front, remained in use for several years (this one was posted in August 1904).

1902 were that the message should be allowed to share the address space, which could be accomplished by printing a dividing line down the centre of the back of the card. The area to the right-hand side of this central line would be for the address and stamp, that to the left for the correspondence. The picture could now entirely take up the other side of the card, without being defaced by any writing. Such a simple idea seemed quite revolutionary at the time, however, and took quite a while to become standard practice. Frederick Hartmann was the first to introduce the 'divided-back' card, yet although the proposal was put forward at the beginning of the year, it seems that such cards were not in circulation until the second half of 1902. Other publishers gradually followed suit, in their own time, but the old-style undivided-back cards appear to have remained in circulation for several

years. Undoubtedly this was partly due to the larger publishers having quantities of the older cards in stock, which they wanted to sell before making up batches of designs with the new divided backs. In addition, the new cards could not yet be used for sending abroad, as the idea had not been adopted by the other member countries of the Universal Postal Union—and would not be for several years. Indeed, it was not until about 1906-7 that divided backs were internationally recognized and generally in use all over the globe.

Both small and large publishing concerns were now producing postcards, either by the handful or in great quantities, using photographic methods. Cards produced in this way could depict their subjects with a down-to-earth realism that the chromolithographic variety did not achieve, and it was not necessary to enlist the printers of Bavaria and

Saxony to get the best results. So the Edwardian card-buying public that scoured the shops for view postcards now generally found themselves with the option of purchasing one of three available types: the real-photographic, the printed photographic, or the artist-drawn card. The first two types, the real-photographic and printed photographic cards, are necessarily linked, for any example of a card whose picture was not originally drawn or painted by an artist must have had its origins in the taking of a photograph. The difference lay in how this photograph was treated to produce the end result.

To look at, the real-photographic postcard appears to be just as its name suggests: it has a glossy finish, the photograph having been developed directly onto a piece of card with a postcard back. In fact, many Edwardian family portraits would come back from the

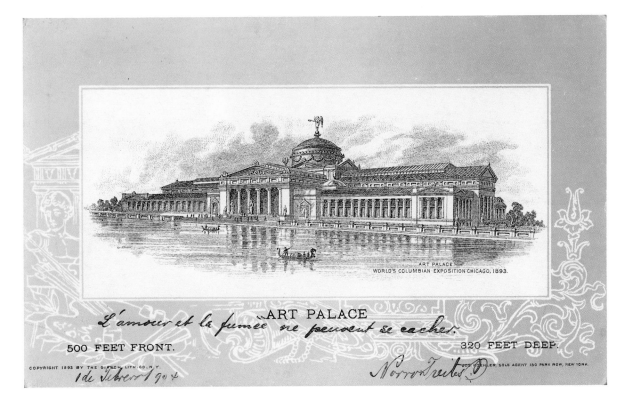

Unofficial view card of one of the many palaces at the World's Columbian
Exposition, Chicago, 1893.

Chromolithographed view of Cairo c. 1905. The card was printed in Germany,
a country which led the field in the production of quality cards using this
technique.

Printed photographic card of St Basil's Cathedral, Moscow's famous landmark, c1902.

11 NEWPORT (Isle of Wight). — Market Day. — LL.

87 EGYPTIAN TYPES AND SCENES. — A Restaurant. — LL.

Isle of Wight market day and Egyptian open-air restaurant, just two of the fine
photographic cards published by Louis Levy.

A Zulu and
his wives,
South Africa.

*American Indian and Zulu
chief with wives. Interest is
growing in 'ethnic' cards
such as these, which depict
native trades and costume.*

photographer's in the form of a postcard, ready for sending to friends and relations. Small photographic companies would keep stocks of such postcard backs for just such a purpose. Indeed, the development of this type of postcard production enabled many village photographers to issue their own cards. In their hands the method's full potential was reached, for it was the local photographer's knowledge that enabled him to capture the type of scenes that are so eagerly sought by today's collectors and historians, scenes of localized interest that were overlooked by the larger publishing concerns.

The local photographer would go out and about in his neighbourhood taking photographs of back alleys as well as high streets and market squares, of the post office and village stores, and of children playing in the street. In fact, the animation of the local people would often prove to be a feature of the photograph, some proudly posing, others shy yet curious of the camera, and those captured while carrying out their trade or profession. The proprietor of the grocer's store may be standing in its doorway, maybe with white-aproned employees alongside if the shop is a larger one; the farm labourer could be snapped while ploughing or reaping; or a photograph could show the farmer's entire family, taken while loading hay onto a horse-drawn cart with pitchforks. Such scenes were the bread and butter of everyday life and yet so often neglected just because of this—except by the local photographer.

Occasionally a special event would take place that would provide an opportunity for some special shots to be taken. The town marketplace may make an interesting photograph in itself, but how much better to capture it during the annual livestock sale. Likewise, a high street is enlivened by photographing it during a carnival procession, and hay-making scenes when the traction engine is at work. Of course, not all special events that made good photos were intentional. Floods, fires, and motor vehicle and train smashes would see the man with the camera on hand to record the evidence; he would hear what had happened and get to the scene before the dust had settled, something the

national publishers could rarely do. The equipment he used had improved a great deal since the 1860s, but was still not the most portable of apparatus; however, he would usually manage to get there for his photographs.

With the photographs safely taken, the next stage was to produce the post-cards. It must be remembered that since most the subjects of these shots were of local interest, the finished card would mainly be of local appeal. The photographer would not expect to sell hundreds and hundreds of each view, and so usually only very small quantities of each were produced. Cards depicting the day to day work of local tradesmen are often found to be the scarcest today, probably because they were the least popular types in their own time. However, maybe two or three dozen or so of a particular scene would be made, the photograph taking up the whole area of the card, since the divided back meant that no space need be left on the front for the written communication. The location would usually be handwritten on the negative and thus appear in white on the finished product. Unfortunately this was not always done, leaving viewers

to guess the whereabouts of the scene in front of them. The cards would then be placed in the local shops for sale, maybe with the photographer's name embossed in the corner or stamped onto the back. However, the great pity is that so many of these photographers of the past remain anonymous to us today, their work in postcard form documenting a bygone era and now keenly sought, but the names of those who created these photographic records of a past way of life unknown.

Real-photographic postcards were also produced by the far larger national firms, but with a difference in subject matter and style. Machines would mass-produce views of high streets in larger towns and cities, the special events, and the rural way of life, but the local traders are rarely to be found on such cards. What can be found are properly set captions as opposed to handwritten ones, often a white border around the photograph, and images constant in clarity and tone—unlike the product of the local man, whose postcards were entirely dependent on his skill as a photographer and developer. Of course, there is a fair bit of variation between

359, Attelage de chiens flamand — Le procès-verbal.

Card showing a laiterie flamande, *or 'Flemish Dairy'. Dog carts are a peculiarity found on a few pre-World War I Belgian postcards.*

Embossed card of the US Capitol, Washington, DC, 1905.

Wheat harvesting in California, a postcard printed in Germany. These days, most collectors of topographical, or view, postcards tend to specialize by only looking for examples depicting the village, town or country in which he or she was born or now lives. Demand for local history material is strong; nostalgia is pushing prices up. Rural activities, such as farming in the days before total mechanization, is just one of the 'social history' categories now much in demand.

216   PARIS. — Le Moulin Rouge. — LL.

The famous Parisian landmark, the Moulin Rouge, published by Louis Levy in 1904. A small proportion of his cards, like this one, were coloured.

Beautiful artist-drawn Italian view, a chromolithograph printed in Berlin.

Painted scene from Raphael Tuck's 'Oilette' series, 'Tennyson Country'.

cards originating from the various types of publishers. Many small firms did indeed manage to give their cards a 'professional' finish, just as many of the larger regional companies were able to publish views with special local appeal. However, in general it is the work of the village photographer, able to capture the social life of a town and its citizens, whose scenes of a bygone age are most valued today.

The printed photographic type of card is any postcard of a photographic origin that does not have that glossy 'real photo' finish to it and that would have been produced by some kind of printed method. Several processes were available to the Edwardian publishers for printing postcards from photographs, all resulting in a matt finish to the end result, and often with a lack of definition when compared to the real-photographic type. Again, the cards tend to fall into local or national categories, although—with the odd exception—the subject matter tends not to be so exciting. Locally published cards more often than not depict views of the village church, the castle,

or some other well-known neighbourhood landmark, the larger publisher again issuing town and city centre streets or endless views of piers, bandstands, and the seafront at popular seaside resorts. Many of these cards were artificially coloured and, as they were printed by machine, tended to be produced in fairly substantial quantities. Tourists being the major purchasers of picture postcards, it can easily be understood that views of seaside holiday towns, cathedrals, abbeys, and picturesque country scenes would sell in large numbers, so such cards tend to be fairly common, even to collectors today. In fact, the great majority of views of any one town are probably going to be of the commoner, printed photographic type; the animated real-photographs are the elusive gems that take time to hunt down.

The number of publishing companies worldwide, both large and small, which issued postcards in the pre-World War era, would run into the thousands, and to describe particular examples here is a fruitless exercise. Several are justly famous in their country of origin for

publishing the finest-quality photographic-view cards and would rightly gain recognition in a more specialized volume than this. However, one such publisher with an international reputation who must be mentioned, is Louis Levy. The printed photographic cards of his French company, recognized by the initials 'LL' after the caption, have a clarity and composition equal to the best real-photographs, even the ones that were hand-coloured, losing nothing in sharpness. Thousands of views of French towns and villages were issued, starting around 1900 with scenes produced for the Paris Exposition, and these were supplemented from 1905 onward by numerous views of London and other towns in southern England. LLs were examples of what could be achieved using the printed photograph; indeed, in France and the rest of Europe this was generally the only method used to produce postcards, where for some reason 'real photos' were rarely issued and are therefore scarce. Continental publishers of course made up for this and their printed photographic postcards are often found to be superior in choice

This novelty hold-to-light German view card, c1904, has cut-out coloured windows that glow when a strong light is placed behind.

Another Raphael Tuck 'Oilette': flower sellers outside the Hôtel de Ville, from the 'Paris' series.

'Large-letter' cards such as this were very popular during the Edwardian period. Whole series of town names, Christian names, and letters of the alphabet were published.

of subject matter and definition—although plenty of dull, unattractive cards do exist!

To the casual observer, however, many of the most attractive view cards are those reproducing, in full colour, the work of the Edwardian landscape artists. Not just a few artists either, but hundreds of them, for the contemporary demand for this type of card meant that painting watercolour views for the publishers was a full-time occupation for many. Reproducing the work of the Old Masters and the great watercolourists of the past was all very well—indeed, Raphael Tuck's first series of cards after the initial 48 London and Thames views were of Turner's masterpieces—but what the public wanted were views of their own country lanes, woodland glades, stately homes, picturesque cottages, and snowy landscapes, more up-to-date and yet keeping that relaxed, timeless quality that made them so easy on the eye: and thanks to the obliging postcard publishers, the public got exactly what it wanted.

The firm of Raphael Tuck was again at the forefront. Tuck's early cards had included series under the 'Rural England' theme, but in 1903 it published the first sets in a series that was to go on for many years, the renowned 'Oilettes'. Under the Oilette trademark faithful reproductions of oil paintings in superb true-to-life colours were issued, usually coming in packets containing a set of six. Watercolours were similarly treated, the finished products going under the 'Aquarette' name. Other publishers joined the fray and soon many artists were especially commissioned to paint these views, in order to satisfy the public's demand. Tuck had the likes of Walter Hayward Young (whose cards were signed 'Jotter'), Henry Wimbush, Charles Flower, and Professor van Hier working for them, although designs by these artists would sometimes be purchased for reproduction by other publishers. J. Salmon Limited had the services of Alfred Robert Quinton ('A.R.Q.') and W. W. Quatremain, whose watercolours, among others, were published over a long period of time in competition to Tuck's. Quinton actually worked for J. Salmon for over twenty years, his published design output easily reaching four figures. On the Continent, the landscapes of Manuel Wielandt were popular, his Italian and French coastal views,

An old fashioned team. Sussex.

Above: This is from Raphael Tuck's 'Rural England' series painted by Harry Payne, who is generally better known for his military artwork.

Right: Delicately coloured scene printed in Leipzig by Meissner & Buch, publishers that established a reputation for their fine range of chromolithographic cards.

Alfred Robert Quinton (1853–1934) was a prolific landscape artist who painted over 2000 designs for postcards during his lifetime. Issued by the publishing firm of J. Salmon, his work first appeared a few years before the First World War and proved so popular that many of his cards were reprinted many times during the 1920s and 1930s. Tranquil country views such as this one are typical of his output.

A landscape by W. W. Quatremain, another member of the team of artists whose work was published by J. Salmon.

Cards such as this superb real-photographic hay-making scene were usually the work of local photographers, and so would have been published only in small quantities.

This card portrays rural life in the early part of the century, cider making in southwest England.

A shopfront with proprietor and staff proudly posing outside. These locally produced cards were often anonymously printed; no photographer or publisher is mentioned on this example.

Anonymously published Edwardian photograph of the staff of a country house; interestingly, it was sent by one of the people in the picture.

Real-photographic street scene with plenty of animation, now highly sought after, by a local publisher in Leeds, 1912. Postcards like this added variety to the output of small publishing firms. Carnivals, markets, fairs, accidents, floods, fires, royal visits—in fact any out-of-the-ordinary occurrence—would usually have the local photographer on hand to record the event, in the hope of selling some of his work later. Many such examples, however, unfortunately carry no clue as to the photographer's identity; the results of their efforts, in the shape of picture postcards, have long outlived them.

printed by chromolithography, beautifully executed.

Raphael Tuck's company soon began to expand its own range of countries depicted. Their Oilettes of America, Europe, the Far East, and Russia were supplemented by the 'Wide, Wide World' series, showing the landscapes, costumes, and customs of a diverse selection of lands spread across the globe. Their cards could indeed be said to look like miniature oil paintings, an effect enhanced by the introduction of the 'Oilfacsim', postcards that were given a textured finish to look and feel like the work of real brush strokes.

Not all the thousands upon thousands of these painted views bore their artists' names. The signatures of the better-known artists appearing on their cards were undoubtedly responsible for many sales, but the medium of the picture postcard was also cause for giving work to many artists of varying talents, whose paintings were eagerly reproduced by publishers desperately trying to keep up with the public's craving for new designs. Such artists would take the moderate fee offered and be happy at that, their identities lost in the rush for publication and only the views of mountainsides, lakes, and meadows they painted living

on in the form of picture postcards.

These, then, were the three basic species of view cards commonly available to the Edwardian public. The printing presses would have churned out their cards in the greatest numbers, so printed views are found to be the most plentiful of the three, with the artist's impressions running a good second. However, the gems of the local photographer who made up his own cards, often depicting the poorer sections of society the others chose to ignore, have in retrospect become the classics of this category.

The pioneering days of aviation were documented on picture postcards, with photographers covering meetings held in their locality. Real-photographic cards showing the brave aviators, the machines in which they performed their feats, the lively scenes at take-off and landing sites during the early air races, were usually printed in limited quantities by these photographers for sale locally, and are now highly prized.

Flower day in Hanover, 1911: an attractive card with chromolithographic panel, posted on the day of the event.

Fine real-photographic card of a mail van, wonderfully detailed and much prized by collectors.

An artist-drawn view with a photographic inset; an unusual combination often used by the Japanese N.Y.K. shipping line for its publicity postcards.

POSTCARDS, POSTCARDS
EVERYWHERE...

Until about the turn of the century, it was possible to keep track of just about all the major postcard issues, the main events that were commemorated, the leading series that were published. Broadly speaking, postcards can be split into one of two groups. There are the 'view' cards (as mentioned in the previous chapter) and there are the 'subject' cards, broadly defined as those that depict something other than a view such as pictures of animals, ships, pretty girls, actors, advertisements, royalty, and so on. There is, of course, some overlapping of the two types: a photograph of an early motor bus in a city street can be classified within the subject of 'road transport' or as a view of the town in which the street is situated. In general, however, the purely 'subject' postcard was still in its infancy as the new century dawned. The *Gruss aus* and court-size vignette views

were still the market leaders. But the subject card was soon to come of age. As the postcard-collecting mania spread across the world, cards were no longer sent purely as holiday souvenirs. Indeed, soon no reason at all was required to mail cards—if it added to the recipient's collection, then that was enough. The public demanded a wider variety of pretty pictures to send, the publishers obliged, and in turn created more demand by issuing a flood of attractive new designs. So it went on, spiralling upward until there seemed to be no end to the availability of picture postcards.

One factor that lent a helping hand to the vogue for postcards was the efficiency of the postal service. Collections were regular, sorting of mail continued at all times (cards bearing Christmas day postmarks are not uncommon), and there were several deliveries per day. Mail

addressed locally would often be delivered within a few hours. With such a cheap, efficient service it is no wonder that the picture postcard became the standard means of communication and the automatic choice for either a quick hello, a birthday greeting, a get-well-soon, a notification of safe arrival and the like.

Although the postcards were of a generally high quality and demand for them prodigious, publishers naturally had a vested interest in keeping things that way. Perhaps the most effective ways of promoting sales of their own product were devised, once again, by Raphael Tuck. Over a period of years this firm held a series of competitions with big cash prizes, each involving the acquisition of Tuck cards by the competitors. In the first of these, which got underway in mid-1900, Tuck was looking for the largest collection of its own postally used cards

The French 'Cocorico' series was one of the rarest of the early sets of cards to be issued. Of the 12 designs in the series, very few turn up today with any regularity.

Two unusual European art cards published shortly after the turn of the century. Both have 'undivided backs' and a token space for a short message on the picture side.

that could be assembled by 25 February 1902. A £1,000 prize was offered, which must have contributed to the increasing interest of card collecting in its early days, and the contest was won by a collection of just over 20,000 cards. A second, similar competition was instigated in 1902, this time £2,000 going to a 25,000-card collection. In 1904–5, contestants were asked to place 300 Tuck cards in their artistic order of merit, and for this a total of £3,000 was offered. Further events on various themes were organized for 1906, 1909, and 1914 (two in this year, one being a painting competition for children).

As if these contests alone were not enough of a boost to the postcard market, Tuck introduced a further incentive to buy by way of its 'proof' postcard editions in 1903. These were deluxe editions of the firm's more important issues, coming in sets of six, each card printed on superior, thicker board with gold bevelled edges and having a protective transparent wrapper. The whole set was presented in an 'artistic portfolio'. Each was limited to 1,000 issues, the sets having consecutive numbers printed upon them and being offered one month in advance of the regular editions. Tuck thought that, by

Raphael Tuck promoted the collecting of postcards in the early days by holding a series of competitions, with big cash prizes for the winners.

1903, postcard collecting had advanced enough to warrant this move, bringing it into line with other branches of the 'art' world where limited editions were regularly issued.

The explosion in the number of cards during the Edwardian era makes the chronological charting of the various issues an impossibility. An idea of some of the typical types of card, with mention of some of the better-known series, is the best that can be hoped for, and any selection is, of necessity, a somewhat personal one. The whole spectrum of printing techniques is to be found at this time, resulting in some of the very best (and a few of the worst) cards ever produced.

The beauty of the picture postcard is that it reflects the society in which it originated. The fads and fashions, the latest inventions, everyday items and products long since obsolete all appear and are proudly depicted with the purpose of appealing to the members of that society —but with a charm that endures to the present day.

During the Edwardian period the postcard was widely used as an advertising medium. It made sense for manufacturers to publicize their products in this

A poster-type advertising card, c1904.

'Like a Flash'; advertisement for the Indian motorcycle, made in Springfield, Massachusetts.

An elegant Edwardian postcard publicizing an elegant Edwardian establishment, the Trocadero Restaurant.

'Racing Colours' published by Wildt & Kray; racing was a sport that crossed all Edwardian class barriers in its appeal.

way, due to the potentially wide circulation these advertisements could have. Just about everything the Edwardian family could want can be found here, such as foodstuffs; non-alcoholic drinks like tea, coffee, and chocolate; beer, wine, and spirits; tobacco; household items such as lamps and sewing machines; and transport-related products (cars, bicycles, tyres, motor oil). Shops, restaurants, and hotels would also advertise their services, from the photographic view of the village stores to the splendid, full-colour artist's impression of the grander city establishments. In fact, a number of manufacturers employed well-known artists of the day to create effective advertisements for them. J. S. Fry, for instance, used the illustrations of Charles Pears, John Hassall, Reg Carter, and Tom Browne to publicize the company's cocoa and chocolate. Many of the finest advertisement postcards are the so-called 'poster-types', again often the work of celebrated artists, but reproducing (or in the style of) famous posters of the period, the works not necessarily having been originally drawn for the postcard. The most famous of these are the Tuck Celebrated Posters series, whose initial cards appeared in

1903. The cards reproduced poster-artwork for a wide range of products, some still around today and some long gone, and included Pear's Soap, Bovril, Schweppes Table Waters, Palethorpe's Sausages, and Bluebell Metal Polish.

Transportation was another subject popular with the Edwardians, and still popular today. Currently, among the most sought-after are the real-photographic cards depicting good close-up views of trams and early motor buses. These pictures were usually taken by a photographer working from a small studio within the vicinity of the route of the particular vehicle shown, and therefore most likely only a handful of cards would have been published. Fire engines, traction engines, and similar unusual modes of conveyance are likewise difficult to find. Far more readily found in old albums, especially those collected by the male of the family, are railway engines, photographs and paintings of which were reproduced in far greater numbers. In the days when there were many small privately owned railway companies and the railway was the chief means of transport, the postcard was readily used to publicize the services of each. Larger concerns,

such as the London & North Western Railway, issued many hundreds of such cards showing their locomotives, carriages (interior and exteriors), trackside features (junctions, signal boxes) and scenic routes. Likewise, the myriad shipping companies extolled the virtues of their lines by depicting their ships on picture postcards, a field difficult for the collector to navigate around due to the multitude of cards issued, some of ships that stayed in service for years, others that literally sank without trace.

Aviation was a theme that caught the public's imagination in the later Edwardian years. Although, very early on in their history, postcards had been carried by balloon (during the Paris siege of 1870), it was not really until Bleriot's channel-crossing of 1909 that flying, and therefore its depiction on cards, became a widespread activity. Photographs of pilots and their machines at the early aviation meetings started to appear in contemporary albums, and, again, these were usually the work of a local firm and thus not produced in great numbers.

There are also some fine artist-drawn cards to be found in the railway, shipping, and aviation categories.

Occasionally cards turn up that were destined to be carried on a special journey and may bear evidence of this in the form of a postmark or commemorative cachet. For example, there are the very rare Lifeboat Saturday issues, which were carried up in a balloon and dropped overboard on special flights to raise money for the lifeboat service in 1902 and 1903; cards that were stamped with a cachet to show that they were carried in an aircraft during the early days of powered flight; and ones with unusual maritime connections, like those posted on the steamships *Columba* and *Iona,* which travelled between Greenock and Ardrishaig in Scotland. These ships offered full Post Office counter services for the passengers, letters and cards thus sent between the years 1879 and 1917 receiving postmarks signifying they had been posted on board.

It can be difficult to comprehend just how powerful the picture postcard was in its heyday or golden age, ie, between the years 1900 and 1914. In the days before television and radio, the postcard was used to change the way people thought about current affairs. It was a political tool, intended for publicity and

One of the very rare Lifeboat Saturday 1903 postcards, which were taken up in a balloon and dropped 'From The Clouds'.

Farman's biplane from Tuck's 'Oilette' series, 'Flying Machines'.

THE SOUTHERN BELLE.
LONDON BRIGHTON & SOUTH COAST
RAILWAY.

In the days before the motorcar had become commonplace, the railways were the main method of travel. Numerous pictures of locomotives and rolling stock were issued, indeed the many railway companies then in existence produced a myriad of designs, each promoting their own services. Today the most highly prized Edwardian railway cards tend to be the 'poster-type' advertising designs, and photographic images of long demolished or much altered small town and village stations.

The Japanese influence, fashionable in late Victorian times, was prevalent in some of Raphael Kirchner's early designs, such as 'Mikado & Santoy' (illustrated) and 'Geisha' series. Many of his other postcard designs dating from the turn of the century are very much in the Art Nouveau style, and were, in the main, published in Vienna, Nuremburg and Paris.

for propaganda purposes, and, depending on the publisher's standpoint, could promote or denigrate the people and policies depicted on it. It was also easily capable of turning those whose photographs appeared on it into stars! In this respect, many politicians, sportsmen, explorers, authors, and musicians achieved passing fame by having their portraits issued on postcards during their moments of achievement. However, nothing was to fare from this latest public craze so well, and to gain so much publicity for itself, as the theatrical profession.

Photographic portraits of actors and actresses started to appear on cards early on in the century, and soon a tidal wave of such cards was being published in Britain, on the Continent, and in America. Without the aid of television, radio and cinema, many theatrical entertainers became celebrities, virtually overnight. Despite the mass-media coverage currently available, these vintage entertainers' names were probably familiar in more Edwardian households than those of all but a handful of leading stars to us today. Leading actresses like Ellen Terry in Great Britain and Ada Rehan in the United States appeared on numerous cards, but it was really the 'pretty young things' of

the latest theatrical fashion, musical-comedy, whose photographs appeared by the thousands in corner shops, high street stationers, and anywhere else a postcard could be purchased. Scenes from just about every West End production could be bought as well as colourful poster reproductions advertising those plays; photographs of their leading ladies and gentlemen in costume, or relaxing at home or with their families, and, of course, the cute, posed head-and-shoulder pictures of the minor stars and chorus girls, many of whom achieved more fame via the postcard than they ever would have done solely through their performances on the stage. In fact, going by the sheer numbers of cards produced, many such actresses must have spent more time in the photographer's studio than they ever did treading the boards. Truly 'superstars' of their own age, they were almost guaranteed to turn up in every Edwardian album.

The theatrical beauties did not, however, have the field all to themselves. They had to compete for the attentions of the public with another type of glamour girl, the type who were dreamt up in the artist's imagination and put down on paper via his palette and brush. The artist-

drawn glamour girl, like the artist-drawn view, often represented an idealized form of reality. She might be elegantly dressed in the height of fashion or wearing little other than a coy smile, but she would always be fair of face and shapely in form.

A wide variety of such cards was published during the Edwardian period. They had started to be issued late in the 1890s on the Continent and quickly found favour worldwide. The work of Raphael Kirchner, an Austrian whose creations were modelled on his wife, Nina, was especially popular and collected all over Europe and America. Cards of a similar style, many depicting pretty young things in various states of undress within their boudoirs, were painted by a number of his contemporaries, the likes of Leo Fontan, Suzanne Meunier, Maurice Millière, Maurice Pepin, and Xavier Sager being among those most highly regarded. The centre of publishing of cards of this type was Paris, although many of Kirchner's designs were issued in his native Vienna and reissued in other countries, too, such was the demand. Such drawings of scantily clad girls were deemed acceptable, whereas photographic cards of nudes were rarely openly on sale and were often confiscated by the Post Office

PHILCO SERIES 7004 F   JOHNSTON & HOFFMANN

Camille Clifford, from a very decorative series of actress postcards by the Philco Publishing Company. Clifford became the embodiment of American cartoonist Charles Dana Gibson's creation, the 'Gibson Girl'. Decorative postcards depicting photographic portraits of actresses abound; thousands upon thousands were issued during the pre-World War I era, in fact in many cases, thousands were published of each of the leading ladies and chorus girls. An interesting and inexpensive field in which new collectors can get involved.

*Four examples from David Allen & Sons'
superb range of theatrical advertising cards.
Theatrical publicity was a subject in which
Allen & Sons specialized and excelled, and the
firm employed leading illustrators of the day,
such as E. P. Kinsella, W. Barribal and John
Hassall.*

*Coquelin on a French hand-tinted photographic postcard.
From 1906 stamps were officially allowed to be fixed to the
'wrong' side.*

if an attempt was made to send them through the mail.

Perhaps because of the more conservative nature prevalent in America and Britain, artists from these countries developed their own, more moderate styles for home publication. Their girls could still be flirtatious, but in a different way. Stocking-clad enchantresses made way for head-and-shoulder portraits of the bright, sophisticated society lady or the demure, innocent, clean-cut girl-next-door type. Series upon series of such cards were issued, with Americans such as Harrison Fisher, F. Earl Christy, Alice Luella Fidler, and Pearl Fidler LeMunyan, and the Canadian artist Philip Boileau,

chiefly responsible for painting them.

Most glamour cards are highly collectible today, despite the large numbers of them which still seem to be around. The most desirable, though, are the earlier examples in the Art Nouveau style, published at the turn of the century just before the postcard craze was established and consequently in much smaller numbers (with their rarity adding to their mystique). These designs have long, flowing, curved lines, and beautiful women surrounded by floral motifs and spirals, giving the overall impression of fluid elegance. Again, they are mostly Continental in origin. The style had all but disappeared by the end of the Edwardian age, but not

before some of the most beautiful cards ever published had appeared. Art Nouveau was the dominant style in several of the important limited-edition series that were issued during the early 1900s, in the tradition of the *Edition Cinos* and *Maîtres de la Carte Postale* series of the 1890s. The French *Collection des Cents* (1901) and *Concours Byrrh* (1906) contained the work of many of the finest exponents of this style, their artistic quality and scarcity making the cards highly sought-after, particularly in the United States and Continental Europe.

Many types or styles of postcard are associated with the country in which they originated. The saucy glamour and Art

s dating from the
ugh these cannot be
, examples of this
ought-after.

Every picture tells a story — although in this case it takes three. French glamour on a fishing theme, c1904.

Pin-up girls by Pera and Ney, published in Paris. Many series of similar scantily-clad girls were issued in that city during the Edwardian and First World War Years.

Nouveau cards are considered typically French; the early view vignettes are associated with Germany (the term *Gruss aus* is still used to cover all such cards); and in Britain the comic postcard grew and thrived like nowhere else. It almost became part of the national heritage—from fat ladies at the seaside to drunks propped up against lampposts, from vicars to amorous young couples. In Edwardian Britain most topics were ridiculed on picture postcards, with nobody, no class of person, no institution safe from the artist's eye. Many of the finest talents were signed up to design these cards. Their illustrations ranged from gently amusing mockery to merciless haranguing of their targets, although, as with the

Oilette view cards, demand was such that many anonymous cards were published to keep pace. It is perhaps curious that many of these retain their comedy today, for although fashions and tastes change, the underlying sense of humour remains the same. At least one can understand what made most of them amusing in their time, although of course there are those whose targets are long forgotten or whose language is dated, which nowadays makes them appear quaint rather than funny, and gives them a different kind of attraction.

Needless to say, it was in the postcard publisher's interests to maintain the public's interest in buying these pictorial pieces of thin cardboard. Although by

1905 there still appeared to be no diminishing of sales (indeed sales seemed to be forever on the increase), certain publishers must have thought that something a little different was required to tempt the jaded postcard-buyer's palate, to give the public an alternative to the endless run-of-the-mill views and pretty pictures normally available. The efforts of some were little more than mere gimmickry, while others must have given much thought to the imaginative issues that resulted. But, either way, a new type of card was found in the shops: the 'novelty' postcard had been born!

Novelty issues can take many forms. The term covers any card that has moving parts or an unusual function, is made of a material other than the usual thin cardboard, has some material or item attached to it, changes in appearance when held in a certain way (usually when held up to a strong light), or is non-standard in size or shape. Made to attract all tastes and suit all pockets, some were very cheaply produced and sold at around the cost of a standard card, while others were quite complicated in their construction and would have been more expensive to purchase.

Looking first at the more elaborate novelty cards that were issued to tempt the public, perhaps the most striking are the so-called 'mechanical' ones. These have moving parts that produce an unexpected and pleasing effect when activated, such as the various kaleidoscope designs published by the Alpha Publishing Company whose revolving wheels cause colour-changing effects within the picture, or those that have a lever to pull in order to make something happen (more often than not of a risqué nature). Although costing more than their straightforward counterparts, such cards were intended to be played with and one would imagine that just about every pair of hands to come across such an example in an Edwardian album would have turned the wheel or pulled the lever. Hence, through wear and tear, such cards in perfect working order are now fairly scarce. Cards with a small gramophone record impressed onto the surface were pioneered at this time, too. The Tuck firm produced over sixteen series of four cards, with each playing a different song at 78 rpm. The same company also introduced the jigsaw-puzzle card, in the form of an Oilette picture on thicker-than-normal board to be pieced together using a standard postcard picture for reference. The gramophone cards seem to be fairly hardwearing ('can be played any number of times', claimed Tuck); the jigsaw-puzzles are scarcer as more often than not pieces went missing.

Various publishers produced cards bearing pictures designed to be cut out and made up into two or three-dimensional models, such as the range of 'dressing dolls' and their clothes, for children to play with. Others issued folding cards with crêpe-paper designs inside that sprang up when opened, or 'squeakers' that emitted a high-pitched bird-imitation type of sound when pressed. Then there are the various 'hold-to-light' cards,

'The Vanities', by W. Barribal. Stylish British glamour, c1912.

A fine chromolithographic card from Meissner & Buch of Leipzig.

'Out on the Deep', humour by Tom Browne, who drew well over a thousand postcard designs during a highly successful, if short, career.

Postcards of animals in human situations are keenly collected these days. This chromolithographic card was published in Great Britain but made in Bavaria.

Left: Typical embossed Thanksgiving greeting, printed in Germany.

Below: Embossed and gilded greetings for George Washington's birthday. The whole spectrum of publishing techniques and types can be found on greetings postcards. Chromolithographs, paintings, photographs, embossing, gilding, appliqué materials; cards for birthdays, Christmas, Easter, Thanksgiving, New Year, Valentine's day — every reason for, and method of, publishing postcards can be found.

These three embossed greetings cards show what American and European publishers could achieve at their best, although some of the cheapest, tackiest cards ever published can also be found within the 'Greetings' category.

Above and right: A selection of novelty cards, including (clockwise): a kaleidoscope, the colours in the peacock's feathers change as the rotating wheel is turned; feathers; a matchstriker; real hair; applied felt; a gramophone record and a leather card.

some of which have a multitude of tiny cut-out windows that glow, others that change from a daytime scene to a night view, and a third type that have a previously invisible second image appearing, all when the necessary illumination is placed behind them.

At the cheaper end of the novelty market, there were cards made of unusual materials such as aluminium, wood, and leather; cards of unusual dimensions ('midget', 'giant', and 'bookmark' sizes); those with an unfolding strip of small views of a particular town tucked away under a flap in the design; and the many appliqué types with some sort of material stuck to the surface and forming a part of the picture. In this latter group can be found head-and-shoulder portraits of pretty girls with real hair attached in the appropriate place, peacocks with real feathers, cards with velvet, lace, and dried flowers affixed to them, and the most basic type, with glitter liberally scattered over the surface. The large numbers of the appliqué types of card that still survive are testimony to the popularity they enjoyed in their prime, but due to some of the difficulties involved in handling them, the post office was not so enthusiastic. Although it cost double to send these novelties, many people appear not to have been aware of this, because examples are often found with postage-due markings. The dangerous nature of the metal cards prompted the authorities to demand that they only be mailed within envelopes. The same instructions were issued for the sending of glitter-covered cards a few years afterward, presumably due to the large amounts of powdered glass that found their way into postbox and sorting-office interiors. The miniature postcards, too, were difficult to handle and resulted in an increase in the minimum allowable size the post office would accept. Tastes eventually change, though, and with a few exceptions the various types of novelty postcard eventually died out. They remain an Edwardian phenomenon that has rarely failed to surprise, and sometimes baffle later generations.

As the Edwardian era drew to a close and the First World War loomed nearer, the postcard craze continued unabated. Just about every subject and view imaginable had appeared on one of these little rectangular pieces of board at some stage in the previous decade or so. They must have had a cheering effect on those

A beautiful children's card by Florence Hardy, published by C. W. Faulkner.

Opposite page left: Appealing American children/greetings card. Publishers followed with interest the progress of the major expeditions of their times. This is H.G. Ponting, photographer with Captain Scott's South Pole Expedition, 1910.

Photographic cards of children, although often appealing, are generally less popular with collectors than fine artistic cards such as the Florence Hardy example above.

who sent, as well as received them, for the messages written on the backs are nearly always found to be of a bright, cheerful nature, despite the hard times that the working classes were having to endure. On looking at the kaleidoscopic variety of these cardboard pictures that was published during this era, it is not so difficult to understand why they had this uplifting effect.

The latest crazes could usually be found on contemporary postcard issues.
During the Edwardian era these included Diabolo, Ping-Pong and Rinking
(roller-skating).

DECLINE AND REVIVAL

The outbreak of the First World War was to see no decrease in the phenomenal numbers of postcards issued by the publishers and bought by the general public. The enormous array of photographs, paintings, and cartoons that had been reproduced in this medium over the previous two decades and more had given the many publishing houses enough experience to be able to adjust to the new circumstances they found themselves in and to produce cards to suit the new moods. Of course, it was no longer possible for British, French, and American publishers to have their cards printed in Germany, but this was not of great consequence, as cheaper colour-printing techniques had for some time been more than adequate to let publication go on unabated at home.

Much of the demand was from the millions of soldiers stationed abroad, who wanted something to send to their loved ones back at home at a time when letter-writing was not always possible. The postcard served as a cheering, quick method of communication in these

SIEGFRIED
Richard Wagner

One from a set of 12 cards depicting characters from Wagner's operas.

A French 'Poisson D'Avril' (1st April) greetings card.

American chic by Harrison Fisher, published by Reinthal & Newman, New York.

difficult circumstances, and the open nature of the correspondence allowed the censor to do his job more quickly, too. But the men at the front did not send back all of the cards they bought. Many were collectors of a sort as well, for they sought out cards depicting the pretty, scantily clad girls who were the product of the more popular artists' imaginations, as a means of temporarily brightening up their surroundings. Picture postcards were the only source of such pin-up material available, and France had a reputation for producing the best of it. Therefore, many such cards, such as those showing semi-naked temptresses in their boudoirs, would have spent the war years adorning the walls of the trenches of Europe and have the pinholes to prove it.

Not surprisingly, however, the main themes prevalent during the years 1914–19 were those of patriotism, propaganda, and sentiment. Despite the atrocities at the front there were still many comic cards as well, observing the humorous side of the war effort. The postcard was initially used as a tool to promote enlistment, for they showed those who did not sign up as being cowards or failures in

A set of six patriotic girls' heads and flags, Italian in origin, by the glamour artist Cherubini. Each is addressed to the same person in Lincoln, England and postally used during January 1916.

Wartime humour to keep up morale of those at the front and those at home.

their various roles in life. National symbols were used extensively to whip up national pride. Flags appeared on vast numbers of cards in those countries actively engaged in the war. There were sets of pretty girls and handsome soldiers dressed in national costume and waving the appropriate national colours, and children shown emulating the grown-ups in outsized uniforms and swamped by flags or banners. Most of these types of cards were painted by artists, some in a straightforward or serious way, others in a much more light-hearted vein. In fact, the humorous angle was to continue throughout the war, because comic cards acted as a tonic to the troops as well as to their families at home. Bruce Bairnsfather was to emerge from the trenches as one of the most famous of these comic artists, remembered for the cartoon character he created, 'Old Bill'. Reg Maurice, Reg Carter, Fred Spurgin, and D. Tempest are just a few of the many others whose comic illustrations helped to keep up the spirits of one

nation during the long years of war.

In addition to these artist-drawn and comic cards, the war years produced their share of factual cards taken from real photographs, these showing the weapons used in combat (tanks, airships, warships), the leaders of the world's fighting forces, and what life was like in the front line. The *Daily Mail* published a long series of Official War Pictures, whose clear images of the weapons in use and events going on at the front were eagerly snapped up at home, often serving as a better guide than any other to the men in the trenches as to what was going on around them. As well as the hardware, the people involved in the war, from royalty to the lowest ranks, found themselves looking out from the surface of picture postcards. In many cases this was nothing new, for cards depicting the royal families of Europe and the leaders of their fighting forces had been fashionable since the mid-1890s. But now, the King and the Kaiser were suitably shown in uniform, and the faces of the admirals

and generals of every country on both sides of the conflict became far more widely known than before. At the other end of the scale, there are many cards to be found typically depicting the low-ranking, yet proud soldier, whose photograph would have been taken by a local photographer, probably at training camp, and made up into a postcard for him. These, of course, never got anywhere near the shops; they were solely done for the benefit of the subject's families and consequently would be treasured far more than any of the professional, nationally published cards could ever hope to be.

The separation of husbands, wives, lovers, and sweethearts caused by the First World War gave rise to a particularly individual type of sentimental postcard: the embroidered silk. Usually made in France, these colourful designs were purchased by the British soldiers stationed there and were sent home. The hand-embroidered messages on the fronts of these were especially chosen with this in

Variation on the suffragette theme, used postally in 1915.

'Old Bill', by Bruce Bairnsfather. This depicts his most-quoted saying 'If you knows of a better 'ole, go to it'.

97. One of our Monster Guns
Official Photograph—Crown Copyright reserved "Daily Mail" War Pictures

120. OBSERVATION BALLOON ASCENDING
OFFICIAL PHOTOGRAPH. CROWN COPYRIGHT RESERVED. "Daily Mail" WAR POSTCARDS

Two of the Daily Mail's *official war pictures, keeping the folks at home informed of events at the front.*

Oilette from Raphael Tuck's 'The European War' series, depicting the French artillery.

mind, for typical of the legends to be found are 'To My Dearest Mother', 'Forget Me Not', 'Thinking of You Always', and 'Home Sweet Home'. More elaborate examples had embroidered flaps covering a small pocket in which a decorative message card could be found; some even had silk handkerchiefs tucked into them. For the less sentimentally minded soldier, similar silk cards could be bought with patriotic messages, flags of the allies, or regimental crests embroidered into them. All these types flourished from 1914 and died out, no longer necessary and unfashionable, during 1919.

The embroidered silk cards were, not unexpectedly, more expensive than normal cards of the period and took a lot out of a soldier's wage packet. Cheaper cards were therefore also required to perform the same function. The soldier in turn needed to be told that the loved ones left behind were still thinking of him. To fulfil these needs, thousands upon thousands of cheap and cheerful sentimental greetings postcards were

published, the majority in Great Britain and France, and mostly of a photographic nature. The posed photographs would typically depict a woman at home with an inset picture of her soldier in uniform conveying an 'I am always thinking of you' message. Variations on the theme would have parents or children in the main picture, but the intent was just the same. On some of these an appropriate verse was printed to convey thoughts that the sender of the card wished to get across but was probably unable to express himself, as for many the war was the first time they had been separated by any great distance and any length of time from the closeness of their families, and so such sentiments had never been written before and did not come easy. Therefore the postcard publishers did the job for them. In a similar vein were the many series of 'song cards' usually found in sets of three or four, each set bearing the words to a well-known song or hymn, one verse to each card. Accompanied by an appropriate posed sentimental photo-

graph to illustrate the verse, cards such as these had been around since the early Edwardian period, but the particular way they expressed feelings and emotions found great favour during the war years.

By the end of the war, the initial enthusiasm, the eagerness to fight, and the combat fever had all but gone. The world had been awakened to the full horrors of global conflict. Many who had been led to believe it would be all over by the first Christmas had had their illusions shattered in the most brutal of ways. For these reasons it could have been expected that the immediate postwar years would have found postcard-publishing houses in a buoyant mood, sharing with the peoples of all nations the celebrations of the cease of hostilities and looking forward to better things to come. In general, however, a more serious mood had swept over everyone and a new age dawned, one in which the frivolities of the postcard did not generally fit. The staggering numbers of cards that had flowed from the publishers' presses

Embroidered silk patriotic and sentimental cards were made in large numbers for the soldiers in France. Some even had inserts, like this silk handkerchief (right).

118

Above: Official German field postcard used in 1915.

Right: Some fine poster-type artwork originated from Germany during World War I and is now keenly collected.

between 1900 and 1918 was now reduced to a trickle: the golden age of the postcard was over.

A further reason for this great drop in the use of cards was that their original, primary function of being a quick, cheap means of communication (as cited way back in the late 1860s) was no longer necessarily true. Due to the war, telephone and radio had been quickly further developed, and, in addition, many nations considerably increased their postage rates, often several times, in the 1918-20 period. The people of the Edwardian age would automatically have turned to the postcard in order to convey a message to a friend; the people of the 1920s had alternatives.

Despite this, all was not doom and gloom on the postcard front. They may have been published in much smaller numbers, but the picture card did not disappear altogether. A fine variety from the 1920s and 1930s can still be found, although it may take a little longer to search them out. Some of the subjects of the cards of this period were the same

popular ones as seen time and time again on pre-war issues. Photographs of royalty and royal events remained a hit with the British public and still do to the present day, as witnessed by the large numbers of 'royal' cards for sale in souvenir shops and at tourist attractions. Sport, too, remained a perennial favourite, with big events such as the Dempsey-Carpentier world title fight of 1921 being well covered. Also, in the United States thousands upon thousands of colourful view cards were turned out depicting the latest buildings in city centres, the tallest office blocks, and interiors of the most impressive restaurants.

The British 'saucy seaside' humorous cards were another type that continued to flourish throughout the 1920s and beyond. The fat ladies squeezed into tight bathing costumes, the vicars, the drunks, and flirtatious young things could be found in the postcard racks at every seaside resort and became so well established that they often prove to be the first type to spring to mind when postcards are mentioned to non-collectors. The

work of Donald McGill typifies this sort of humour, and in fact in many ways he 'is' seaside comedy. His designs were keenly bought from the time he started drawing postcards in 1904, but his most prolific period was 1914-1950, when he drew literally thousands of these cartoons (although the later ones suffered from poor-quality printing). Other artists were to find success with particular cartoon creations that caught on in a big way. George Studdy came up with Bonzo, a naughty puppy who attained cult status and appeared on cards the world over, as well as causing other spin-off products such as ceramic Bonzos and soft-toy Bonzos. Lawson Wood likewise created Gran'pop the chimpanzee. And then there were the 'film-star' cartoon characters that appeared on many postcards by popular demand, such as Felix the Cat

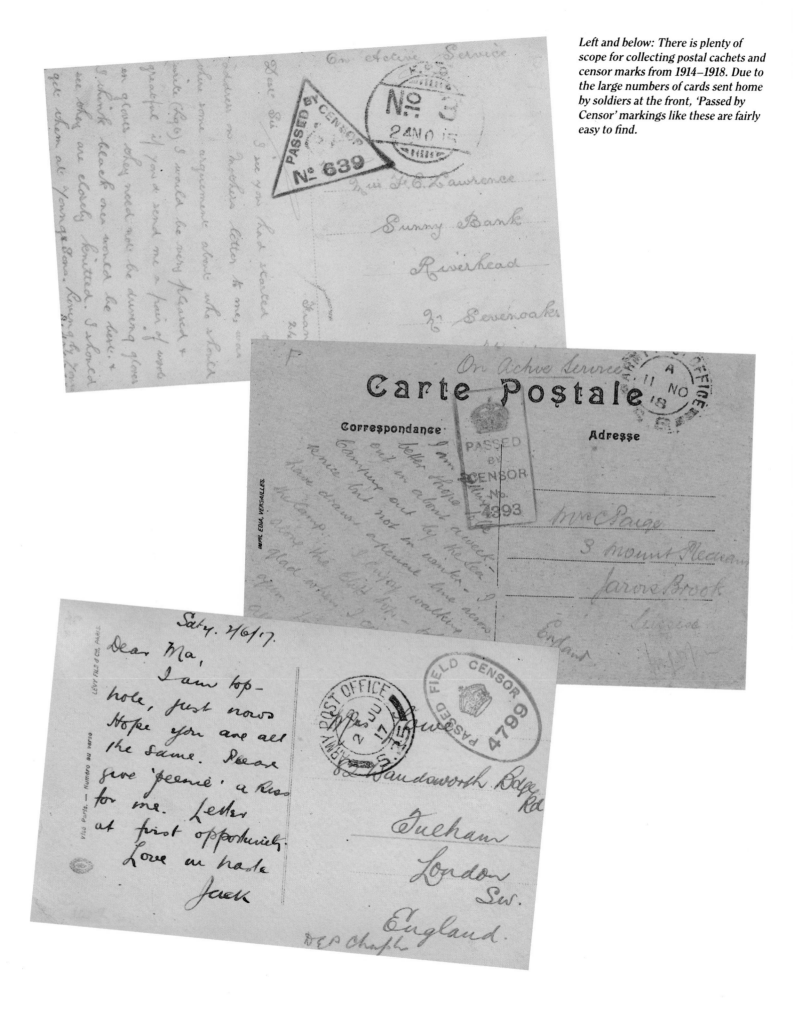

Left and below: There is plenty of scope for collecting postal cachets and censor marks from 1914–1918. Due to the large numbers of cards sent home by soldiers at the front, 'Passed by Censor' markings like these are fairly easy to find.

Left: The latest fashion, as drawn by Flora White. The picture postcard mirrored the changes in fashion from the Edwardian age, with the latest 'thing' usually depicted in a gently amusing manner.

WARTIME ECONOMY

"Economy in Clothes!"

More wartime humour, this time from Donald McGill, whose prodigious output was more often of the 'saucy seaside' type. Much postcard humour was of a topical nature, with current events providing the themes for the artists to work on.

"POOR MAN! AND HAVE YOU BEEN WOUNDED AT THE FRONT?"
"NO, MA'AM —— AT THE BACK!"

and the various Walt Disney creations.

Indeed, film stars (real life ones) were to figure prominently on cards of the 1920s and 1930s and, like their Edwardian theatrical predecessors, were eagerly collected by their fans at the time. From the days of the silent screen, new stars to emerge in Hollywood were publicized by having their photographs appear on the film companies' cards, although such issues usually came with a rather dull sepia finish. The best cinema photographs were to appear a little later, in series such as the one published by *Picturegoer* magazine. The Picturegoer cards featured top-quality, glossy head-and-shoulders portraits of all the leading actors and actresses, as well as series of Film Partners and Film Scenes. Radio, and later, television stars joined the comprehensive range, supplementing the choice available. However, despite their unquestionable popularity, cinema cards of the 1920s-30s were not published in quite the enormous quantities that Edwardian theatrical cards had been, although through the medium of the film, most of the bigger names are better remembered.

Perhaps the most stylish, colourful

224   THE TRIBUNE TOWER, BY NIGHT, CHICAGO

Above and right: According to the backs of these cards, the Tribune Tower is 'the most beautiful office building in the world', and the Roosevelt Hotel 'the largest and finest in the South'.

postcards to emerge during that first postwar decade were those painted by the devotees of the latest artistic fashion, Art Deco. The Art Deco movement had been gaining followers since the Edwardian era, but suddenly the style spilled over into everyday life in the mid-1920s with clothing, furniture, and household gadgets and utensils following the fashions of bold, bright colours and geometric shapes. Because postcard publishers have always followed and documented the fashions of the day, designs in the Art Deco style naturally appeared on their products. Some fine sets of children's cards and nursery rhymes were issued, by artists such as Joyce Mercer, C. E. Shand and Henriette Willebeek Le Mair, while well-designed, yet anonymous, greetings cards also could be found. As far as the postcard was concerned, however, many of the best designs were to fall within the 'glamour' category, and it was the Italian artists who seemed to excel here. The names to be found beneath some of the stunning, stylized artwork are those of Umberto Brunelleschi, Carlo Chiostri, M. Montedoro, Tito Corbella, G. Meschini, Adolfo Busi and Achille Mauzan, among others. The

The ROOSEVELT
NEW ORLEANS
"The Pride of the South"

Right: Of all the series featuring film stars, the 'Picturegoer' cards were among the best. Their publicity leaflet stated 'These portraits, all real photos, latest poses, superb glossy finish, will bring you joy through the years. And as new stars twinkle they are added to our selection. So take this opportunity to swell your collection to start a thrilling new hobby'.

I'LL BE LOOKING YOUR WAY SOON!

Above: George Studdy's Bonzo appeared on numerous cards and became an international hit. He appeared on issues from America, Holland, France and Germany shortly after his debut in Britain in the early 1920s, and proved to be so popular that many other spin-off products were sold as well. This popularity continued right up to his creator's death in 1948, and has been rekindled by the current wave of Bonzo collectors.

Right: Felix the Cat, star of the silver screen and the postcard. Created by Pat Sullivan, an Australian artist, a photographic portrait of him even appeared in the famous 'Picturegoer' series of film-star cards.

HER WINDOW!

ERROL FLYNN

OLIVIA DE HAVILLAND

DOUGLAS FAIRBANKS & MARY PICKFORD

JANE RUSSELL

UNITED ARTISTS

Holland-America Line. t.s.s. **STATENDAM**. 28291 tons register - 38950 tons displacement

Holland-America Line advertising card. Shipping remains a favourite subject with many collectors.

majority of their designs were published in their native country and include some genuine classics, which are now highly prized and very expensive. Yet the Italians did not have the field all to themselves, as stylized floral themes and vivid colours featured to a lesser extent in issues published elsewhere with Mela Koehler, Annie French and Chilton Longley among the leading exponents.

By the mid-1930s Art Deco was dying out. Another world war was on the horizon and getting ever nearer. Of course, postcard publication was to continue during the 1939-45 era, but the numbers produced were nowhere near the considerable quantities of 1914-18. One reason why these later issues can be quite difficult to come by today, in addition to their relative shortage, is that at the time they were published postcard collecting was no longer the great national pastime it had been 25 years earlier. Whereas pre-1918 cards had been collected by the albumful, this was

not the case in 1940, so Second World War cards tend to crop up individually in odd places, rather than in bulk lots or large original collections.

As during the previous conflict, postcards depicted the forces of land, sea, and air, the personalities in charge of operations, the heroes and the villains. The humour was still there, with children often drawn making light of the latest situations such as the carrying of gas masks, the queueing for rations, and the enforced blackouts. The work of Mabel Lucie Attwell, whose cute children had been selling well since before World War I, was still in evidence, the situations they found themselves in appropriately updated. This time around, most of the glamour was to come from America, although the artist-drawn pin-ups were far fewer than before as photographs of real-life beauties, such as Hollywood's leading ladies, were now the favourites. However, perhaps some of the best postcards of the era were the official

issues of Germany. Some fine coloured poster-type artwork promoting events held in that country at the time of the Third Reich can be found, much of it promoting the Nazi creed. Plainer, one-colour official cards were frequently issued during the 1930s to get across the National Socialist message within Germany, commemorating events such as Hitler's birthday and the Nuremberg Rallies. These cards were usually larger than standard size and were often given additional interest by the use of appropriate commemorative postmarks. The postcard and postage stamp were also widely used in Germany to raise money, with many issues carrying a supplementary charge that went toward Hitler's Culture Fund or the Winter Relief Fund.

The Second World War, then, inspired a certain amount of publisher interest at the time, and today it commands a fair degree of retrospective collector interest, certainly for the military issues. The same, however, cannot be said of

Charming 'fairy' card by Molly Brett, published by C. W. Faulkner.

Art Deco romances by Corbella , Colombo and Meschini, printed in Italy.

the issues of the following two decades. During the 1950s and 1960s the picture postcard was most definitely out of fashion; the products of these years are generally regarded as the nadir of the postcard's history. Original, creative cards were not produced due to lack of interest from the publishing houses, and the public had an ever-widening number of ways to fill up their leisure time, television being one of the main ones. General views, holiday attractions, and national events were still covered, yet the cards had an uninspiring look about them, and a cheap and cheerful 'make-do' approach seemed to be taken that hardly attracted people to buy, keep, and collect them. Despite this, nowadays it can be worth keeping an eye open for these 'unwanted' cards. Sometimes advertisements, the transport of the period, and occasionally the fashions can be found and picked up extremely cheaply, far more cheaply than their rarity should warrant. The more interesting examples are generally much scarcer than their equivalent Edwardian issues, yet are usually a fraction of the price. But this could always change, since the cheap cards of today can easily become the expensive ones of tomorrow, especially when the subjects depicted fall within a popular category.

The late 1960s marked a revival in the fortunes of the picture postcard. Not only did the collecting of Edwardian cards once again start to become a popular pastime, but the re-emergence of the publishing of quality designs was also noticeable. This was a trend that continued, so that by the late 1970s postcard publishing was again firmly established at a level not seen since the end of the First World War, and was to go on from strength to strength throughout the 1980s. Some of the subject matter of the modern-day issues was the same as the cards of old, but with the themes developed for modern-day tastes. Glamour, for instance, has become perhaps the most sought-after category. A set of twenty glamour cards by the artist Aslan (published 1968-70) started the ball rolling and now fetches around £100 ($200) for the set. Many further superb cards have since followed, the work of a new generation of photographers and artists, some of which are undoubtedly destined to become the classics of the future. Other popular themes of old still strongly in

Above and below: Greetings in the Art Deco style from Germany and Poland.

A superb set of six early stylized Art Deco glamour cards by M. Montedoro. Along with that of Umberto Brunelleschi, Montedoro's work epitomized Art Deco at its finest, an explosion of clashing colours, geometric shapes and a classical style. The majority of designs such as these were the works of Italian artists, published in their native country—apparently in fairly small quantities, for examples of this quality are very rare and consequently very expensive. If they can be found, expect to pay well into three figures for such a set.

Postcards catering for all tastes can be picked up at the various fairs and auctions, now regularly held just about everywhere. Top left is a 'Fantasy Head': the portrait of composer Franz Liszt is made up of naked figures! The Olympic (top right) was sister ship to the Titanic. Of the many cards issued after the latter's sinking, several were actually doctored views of this liner. Advertising, military, social history and animal postcards can all also be found amongst the many other subjects in dealer's boxes.

This whopping fish I caught to-day,
I got him on the shore,
And if he doesn't get away
Next mail I'll send you more.

This shows his monster fins,
As big as any sail;
You'll get another card from
And then you'll have his ta

COPYRIGHT, 1906.
THE WILDWOOD POST CARD CO.
WILDWOOD, N.J.

THE FISH STORY

Greetings and Comic postcards were amongst the most prolific types produced during the postcard's heyday, and are therefore widely available today. Just about every occasion and subject was featured, although there are still gems to be found such as this fish story. Composite sets such as this were designed to be sent, one at a time, on successive days, until the recipient had the complete picture. However, there was still the problem of how to display such a set in the family album!

His tail it lashed the briny sea,
I dropped my line to run,
And then he got away from me,
And thus my story's done.

NOW THAT FATHER'S
SHAVED HIS WHISKERS OFF, AND
MOTHER WEARS A HAREM SKIRT,
HOW CAN I TELL WHICH IS WHICH?

I'M TOO BUSY TO WRITE.

demand include film stars, animals, royalty, transport, and sporting cards.

However, there are several new themes brought about by developments in technology and changes in fashion that were not available to our Edwardian predecessors, and which are introducing new generations to what the postcard has to offer. Space exploration, science fiction/fantasy, television tie-ins, and all branches of pop music (rock, punk, heavy metal, and all their variations) are selling in enormous quantities in art and poster shops, newsagents, galleries, and souvenir shops all over the world. The use of the airbrush, advanced photographic equipment, and modern printing techniques are also reflected in today's highly creative, well-produced postcards, making them worthy of examination by all budding collectors. However, these current issues fundamentally differ in one particular respect from those of ninety years ago, in so much as the reason they are published has fundamentally changed.

At the beginning of the twentieth century, even though cards were intended to appeal to collectors, their chief function was still as a means of communication. Many would have been bought to be kept by the purchaser and go straight into his album; however, they were there primarily to be written on and posted. Not so today, however, for most of the postcards found in the racks of shops, galleries, and museums these days, other than the holiday-view types, will never see the inside of a postbox. They are aimed chiefly at the collector market. Quite a few are in fact published in limited editions, which will not reach general circulation in any case, but are sold by specialist dealers to specialist collectors, never to be postally used.

At least the current market gives the new collectors of today a chance to purchase quality cards as they appear at nominal cost, where shrewd buys could see a reasonable increase in value in the future. It could likewise pay to search out and carefully select the better issues of the 1950s and 1960s, currently a very depressed era of postcard history. Older issues, those of pre-1920s vintage, have been sought by collectors since the resurgence of interest in postcards in the late 1960s, and so prices have had time to build up and find their own levels. Even so, postcard collecting is still a relatively cheap hobby. The vast majority

'La Promenade', an Art Deco card by Rie Cramer.

'The Queen of Hearts', by Randolph Caldecott. Forty-eight of Caldecott's nursery rhyme illustrations, many originally drawn for Victorian children's books, were reproduced in postcard form by F. Warne in c1930.

Exhibitions continued to be a popular subject with publishers in the first half
of the twentieth century; this one is for a philatelic event in Algeria, 1930.

Photographic card of the Titanic leaving Southampton on her fateful maiden
voyage, 10 April 1912. Possibly the most famous incident of Edwardian times,
the disaster brought about a number of commemorative and 'in memoriam'
postcards, but pre-sinking photographs like this are much scarcer. Should the
postmark and message prove that the card had been written and posted on
board, the added interest from shipping enthusiasts could push the value
sky-high.

GOLDEN GATE BRIDGE LOOKING TOWARD TREASURE ISLAND ON SAN FRANCISCO BAY

Another exhibition card from the 'Golden Gate International', San Francisco, 1939.

can be picked up for between 50p and £5 ($1–$10) each, many at the bottom end of this price range.

At the other end of the spectrum, very, very rarely an exceptional card may sell at auction for a four-figure sum, but when this occurs there may be other factors influencing the price, pushing it up way beyond the normal value of the card itself. To take a couple of examples, a photographic portrait card of an eminent personality, Winston Churchill for instance, would on its own only be worth a nominal sum, that is, a few pounds or dollars. But if that card were signed by the subject (and Churchill's autograph is highly prized), the value would shoot up a hundredfold. However, it would be autograph hunters, rather than postcard collectors, paying the higher sum in order to obtain the signature; the fact that it is

on a postcard is almost incidental. Likewise, a card depicting the *Titanic* may ordinarily be worth around £25 ($50), but suppose it had been written on board ship as she set sail from Southampton and posted at the first mail drop a couple of days before the famous sinking this would make the card far more interesting, a real gem for Titanic enthusiasts and shipping historians; its value correspondingly goes through the roof. In this case it is the circumstances in which the postcard was used that causes the high price tag. Other instances of the use of a card inflating its value would include 'flown' items with appropriate postmarks or cachets, cards used on the first day of issue (the first Austrian *Correspondenz-Karte* of 1869, postally used on the day of issue 1.10.1869, would be worth a few hundred pounds, for example), and

those sent from important expeditions (eg, the Scott 'Links of Empire' set mentioned previously).

In most instances, though, postcards that sell for £50-100 ($100-200) would be the cream of the crop, and may include the very best Art Nouveau and Art Deco specimens, examples from some of the rare Continental 'collections' (such as the *Editions Cinos, Cocorico, Concours de Byrrh* and *Wiener Werkstätte* series), the finest early close-up photographic transport cards (motor buses and trams), and exceptional social-history photographs. The latter two groups are most popular in Great Britain, with prices for the best street scenes, agricultural and industrial photos, disasters, and events on the increase, whereas in America and on the Continent it is the better 'art' and 'subject' cards that are most in demand. Even so,

Official issue for the 1936 Olympic Games held in Berlin (although the actual events commemorated on this card took place in Kiel). The card also bears one of the special pictorial cancels.

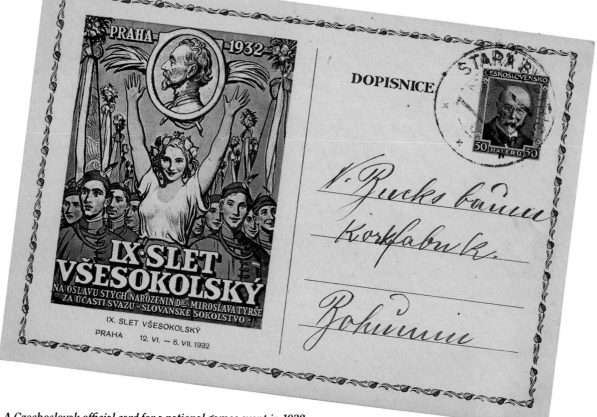

A Czechoslovak official card for a national games event in 1932.

Left: Superb Italian Fascist Party propaganda postcard.

German official 'Welfare Fund' card depicting the bust of President Hindenburg, 1933.
In addition to the six-pfennig postage, a further four-pfennig for the fund was added.

Left and below: Products and events of the present are well publicized by a range of modern advertising cards.

FREE CATALOGUE · FREE DELIVERY · FREE CREDIT — WHY WAIT?

STREETS OF LONDON
FREEPOST 11
OXFORD STREET
LONDON W1E 5EY

when some of the finest postcards the hobby has to offer can still be picked up for double figures (pounds or dollars), they have to be considered cheap, especially when compared to other branches of collecting (stamps, books, ceramics, etc), where items regularly sell for hundreds, thousands, and even tens of thousands.

However, the postcard collector does not even need to spend double figures on his or her purchases. As mentioned previously, less than £5 ($10) will secure any number of excellent photographic and art designs in practically every category, and these can be picked up from the ever-growing number of specialized postcard fairs now held almost everywhere. These fairs are usually well attended by specialist dealers, whose stocks will be laid out and sorted by subject, artist, locality, and country, thus saving a lot of time for those with specific interests. Postcard auctions, too, offer cheaper cards in small groups or collections, as well as better cards sold individually, thus catering for the specialist and beginner alike, so whatever the depth of his or her pocket, the postcard collector will nearly always be able to find something of interest. Now established as one of the world's favourite collectibles, the postcard is once again grabbing public attention. Things have come a long way since that first, small rectangular piece of brown board appeared in Austria in 1869.

Left: Every year since 1979, the BIPEX postcard fair has been accompanied by an attractive promotional issue. 'Postcards about postcards' have long been popular with collectors.

BIPEX 1986
17th - 20th SEPTEMBER

QUEUE HERE FOR BIPEX

A PLETHORA OF PICTURE POSTCARDS TO MAKE YOU PURR!
AT THE NEW TOWN HALL, KENSINGTON, LONDON.

Transport-related postcards have always been popular with collectors. It is one of the few categories to have been strongly in evidence throughout the last 90-or-so years of card publishing, with each decade offering its share of issues. The 1970s and 1980s have seen enormous numbers of photographs of historic modes of conveyance issued to add to this selection, with practically every museum involved in restoration and preservation selling souvenir cards to visitors.

» Focke-Wulf F W 200 Condor «

The 1960s and early 1970s are a neglected era of the postcard's history, most examples from this period can still be picked up very cheaply. Good, social history cards such as this fire brigade turnout are already becoming difficult to find today and could become expensive in years to come as the sixties are 'rediscovered' from the postcard point of view.

Bands may come and bands may go, but current favourites are always keenly collected. Photographic portraits, posters, album covers, and live shots can all be found reproduced on 'rock & pop' postcards.

The Great Events. These two cards are from a series by Nugeron depicting memorable events in recent history. The examples here would be additionally collectable because they fall into other popular categories, namely Space and Glamour/Monroe which are keenly collected in their own right. Social history cards that cross the boundaries into other themes, like these, will usually attract a small premium due to the additional number of thematic collectors looking for them.

1962 - AUGUST THE 5th MARILYN MONROE DEAD

1969 - FIRST HUMAN BEING ON THE MOON

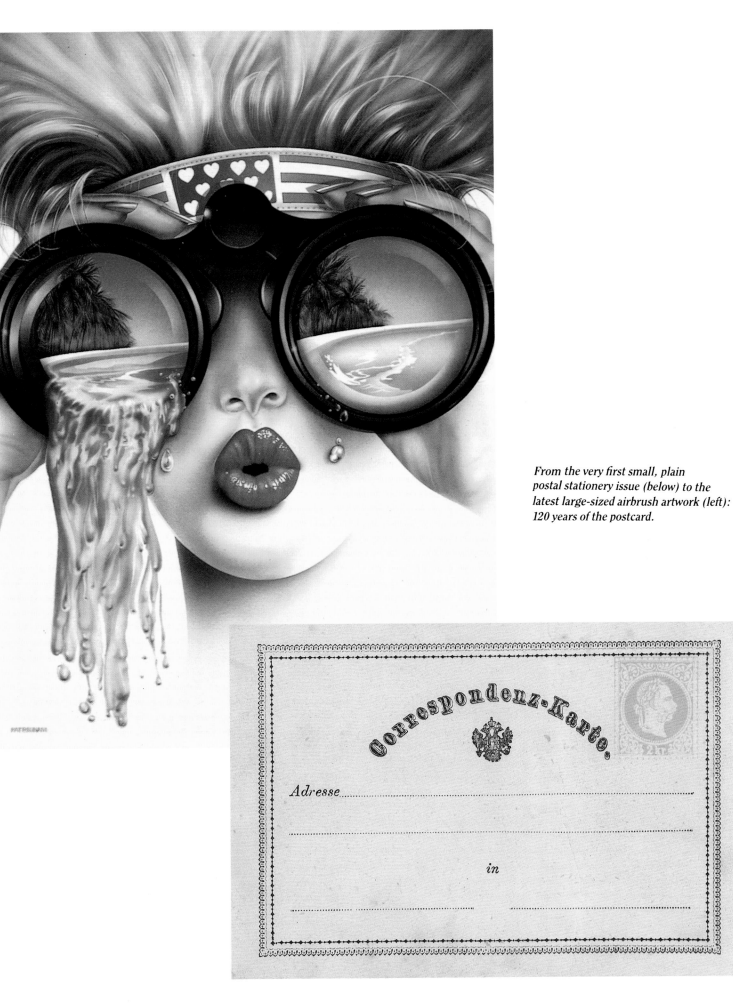

*From the very first small, plain
postal stationery issue (below) to the
latest large-sized airbrush artwork (left):
120 years of the postcard.*

COLLECTING POSTCARDS

The best place to purchase postcards of all ages is often at one of the many fairs held regularly at an ever-growing number of locations. Here specialist dealers bring along and lay out their stocks, so collectors can buy, sell and exchange.

It is worth checking local press for events, but on a larger scale the following two specialist postcard fairs in England are recommended, with over a hundred dealers and thousands of collectors in attendance to ensure an enjoyable, bustling atmosphere. Check *Picture Postcard Monthly* for dates on these and other fairs:

> British International Postcard Exhibition (BIPEX)
> Kensington Town Hall, London
> Large 4-day fair held annually in early September
>
> IPM Promotions Bloomsbury Fair
> Royal National Hotel, Woburn Place, Bloomsbury, London WC1
> Held monthly on Sundays

Auction Houses which have regular specialist sales of picture postcards include:

> Garnet Langton, Burlington Arcade, Bournemouth, England BN1 2HY
>
> Phillips West Two, 10 Salem Road, London, England W2 4BU
>
> Specialised Postcard Auctions, Corinium Galleries, 25 Gloucester Street, Cirencester, Glos., England GL7 2DJ
>
> T. Vennett-Smith, 11 Nottingham Road, Gotham, Nottingham, England NG11 0HE

BIBLIOGRAPHY

For those wishing to take up postcard collecting, or to learn more about them, the following are recommended reading:

The Picture Postcard and its Origins, Frank Staff (Lutterworth Press, London, 1966)

Picture Postcards in the United States, 1893–1918, G. & D. Miller (C.N. Potter, New York, 1976)

Collecting Postcards, 1894–1914, V. Monahan & W. Duval (Blandford Press, Poole, Dorset, 1978)

Picture Postcards and their Publishers, A. Byatt (Golden Age Postcard Books, Malvern, Worcestershire, 1978)

Picture Postcards of the Golden Age, T. & V. Holt (Postcard Publishing Co., 1978)

Picture Postcards and Travel, Frank Staff (Lutterworth Press, London, 1979)

Collecting Postcards, 1914–1930, V. Monahan & W. Duval (Blandford Press, Poole, Dorset, 1980)

An American Postcard Collector's Guide, V. Monahan (Blandford Press, Poole, Dorset, 1982)

Picture Postcard Artists, T. & V. Holt (Longman, London, 1983)

Till The Boys Come Home – Picture Postcards of the First World War, T. & V. Holt (Longman, London, 1983)

Annually-published postcard catalogues with comprehensive price guides include:

RF Picture Postcard Catalogue, compiled by R. Mead, J. Venman & D. Brooks, RF Publications, Rayleigh, Essex.

IPM Catalogue of Picture Postcards and Year Book, compiled by J.H.D. Smith, IPM Publications, Lewes, Sussex

A monthly publication with articles, news items and listings of forthcoming events on the postcard scene; also dealer, auction and postcard fair advertisements:

Picture Postcard Monthly (ed. Brian Lund), 15 Debdale Lane, Keyworth, Nottingham, England NG12 5HT.

INDEX